The Next Right Step

How to Move Forward at Midlife When You Look Successful
But Feel Stuck

Robby Allen

2026

Contents

Copyright

Dedication

For the coaches and mentors who showed up for me on muddy fields and in cockpits, and for the boys and young men I have tried to show up for since.

———————————————

A note from the author

This is not a productivity book. It is not a wellness manual. It is not a Stoicism rehash, a "second act" reinvention guide, or a motivational self-help book about manifesting the version of yourself you have been waiting to become.

This is a book for adults whose lives are, by every external measure, working — and who suspect, in the kitchen at 5:47 a.m., that something underneath has stopped.

You do not have to be in crisis to need this book. Most readers are not. Most readers are, by every visible measure, *fine* — finished with one role, not yet sure of the next, and quietly carrying the question of what the rest of the years are for.

The book is a system for that.

I am a former Marine Corps officer and F/A-18 pilot. I left the uniform some years ago. The transition, like most transitions, took longer than I expected and went in directions I did not anticipate. The book draws on what I learned, on what I have watched several hundred other men and women learn, and on the small framework that emerged out of those years.

A note on how to read it: read it once to get the shape. Then keep it nearby. The chapters are designed to land harder the second time.

The promise of the book: by the time you finish it, you will have moved.

Begin.

Introduction — The Uniform Comes Off

The clock on the microwave reads 5:47 a.m. Renee is in her kitchen, in the same robe she's worn every morning for fifteen years, drinking coffee from the mug her old VP gave her two Christmases ago. The mug says CHIEF MARKETING OFFICER in white block letters across the side. She still uses it. She is aware this is a problem.

She has been a former chief marketing officer for nineteen days.

She knows the number because she counts. Nineteen days since the conversation in the small conference room. Nineteen days since the email to the team she'd built. Nineteen days since the badge — the actual physical badge, the one she wore on the lanyard, the one she kept clipped to her belt during all-hands meetings even though no one needed her to scan in to anything anymore — went into the drawer next to her passport. She still goes to the drawer sometimes. She tells herself she is looking for the passport.

Her phone is face down on the counter. She doesn't pick it up. There isn't anything to pick it up for. The Slack notifications stopped on day two. The calendar invites stopped on day three. The "let's get a drink soon!" texts kept up for about a week and then thinned to one or two stragglers from people she didn't actually want to drink with. The world, it turns out, loves a CMO and is not very interested in a former one.

She sits down at the kitchen table. She has nowhere to be. Nothing requires her presence. There is no meeting that will start without her. There is no Q4 deck that will go to the board with a missing slide if she does not open her laptop in the next forty-five minutes. She is, in the language of the LinkedIn profile she has not yet updated, *exploring her next chapter.*

She has no idea what her next chapter is.

She sets the mug down. She looks at her hands. She has the strangest physical sensation, which is that her body is still trying to lead. There is nothing to lead. The body has not received the memo.

This is not the part of the story she thought she would be writing.

Renee is fifty-one years old. She is, by every external measure she would have used at thirty-five to define a successful life, successful. She has the house. The marriage that took work but worked. The kids who turned out fine. The retirement account that means she does not, technically, ever have to work again. The friends who would show up if the house caught fire. The reputation, the references, the contact list of people who answer when she calls.

And yet at 5:47 a.m. on a Wednesday in early March, she is sitting alone in her own kitchen, in her own robe, holding her own mug, counting days since something ended.

She is not depressed. She has been depressed once, in her thirties, and this is not that. She is not having a midlife crisis. She is too old, frankly, and too tired, and not nearly dramatic enough. She is something quieter, something for which the language is bad. The closest word in her vocabulary is *stuck.* But "stuck" doesn't quite get it. Stuck implies she has been trying to move and failing. She has not been trying. She doesn't know what she would be trying *toward.*

She is in the room after the room.

If you are holding this book, you might not be Renee. You might not be a former CMO. You might be a former vice president, a former senior director, a former managing partner. You might be a former parent — your youngest left for college twenty-six days ago and the silence in the house is not the relief you had been promised. You might be a former founder, six months past the acquisition, watching the new owners run your company differently and unable to say anything about it. You might be a former teacher, a former pastor, a former coach, a former cop, a former first sergeant. You might be a person who never wore a uniform anyone could see, but who wore one nonetheless, for so long that it stopped feeling like clothing and started feeling like skin.

You took the uniform off. The skin did not grow back.

That is where this book begins.

———————————

Here is the claim this book is built on, and I am going to make it on page two, because it is the thing you most need to hear and the thing every other book in this section will spend three hundred pages working up to:

This is not a midlife crisis. It is a midlife transition. And the reason you cannot find your way out of it is that you are waiting for the wrong thing.

You are waiting to feel ready. You are waiting for clarity to arrive. You are waiting for the next thing to "speak to you." You are waiting for inspiration, for passion, for some quiet voice inside that is supposed to tell you what to do with the rest of your finite, unfinished life.

It isn't coming. Or rather: it is coming, but not in the order you have been told to expect.

In the order you have been told, clarity comes first and action comes second. You figure out who you are, then you act on it. You find your passion, then you follow it. You feel ready, then you move.

In real life, in the lives of every adult I have watched move forward through transitions like the one you are in right now, the order is reversed. Action comes first. Clarity follows. You move, and the movement tells you what comes next.

The reason this book exists is because no one tells you that.

A quick word about what this book is not, before we go further.

This is not a book about depression. If you are in a clinical depression, the most loving and direct thing I can tell you is to put this book down and call your doctor, and pick it back up when you have stabilized. The two are different problems and require different interventions. Don't mistake one for the other.

It is also not a book about burnout. If your stuckness is your body screaming at you to rest, what you need is rest, not a book full of ideas about forward motion. The body is reliable on this point even when the mind is not. You will know which is which.

It is also not a book about grief. If your role ended because someone you loved died, or because a marriage you wanted ended, or because the version of you who used to wake up in this kitchen has been slowly disappearing for reasons you cannot yet name, you may need a grief book before you need this one. Grief has its own work and its own pace and its own architecture, and the framework in this book — built for forward motion — will not, by itself, hold the kind of weight that grief carries. Two suggestions, if that is where you are. First, give the grief its time. The framework will still be here. Second, find a grief book; *On Grief and Grieving* by Elisabeth Kübler-Ross and *The Year of Magical Thinking* by Joan Didion are reasonable starting points. Some readers will be in both places at once — actively grieving and ready to start moving. That is a real position. The framework can run inside grief, on the slower of its possible cadences, but it cannot replace the grief work, and pretending it can usually means the grief work surfaces later, larger, and more urgent than it would have if you had let it have its time first.

What this book is for is the much more common and much less

discussed state of having lost the structure that organized your forward motion, without yet having found the next one. You are, technically, fine. The body is fine. The bills are paid. The people you love are alive. The structure is gone. The room is empty. And you do not yet know what to do with your hands.

If that is where you are, you are in the right place.

––––––––––––––––––

I am going to be direct with you, because I think you have been talked down to by enough self-help books for one lifetime.

This book is not going to ask you to find your purpose.

It is not going to ask you to manifest your best self, design your ideal day, or imagine your funeral and reverse-engineer your life from there. It is not going to give you a forty-page worksheet about your values. It is not going to tell you to wake up at four a.m., journal for an hour, and meditate before checking your email. It is not going to promise you that the next chapter will be more meaningful than the last one if you only follow these seven principles.

What this book is going to ask you to do is much smaller and much harder.

It is going to ask you to take the next right step.

Not the next big leap. Not the next strategic pivot. Not the next bold reinvention. The next *right step*, which is the small, specific, defensible thing your future self will not have to fix. It is going to ask you to take that step today, even though you do not feel ready, even though you do not know where you are going, and even though the people who say they love you are giving you helpful advice about finding your passion that is making everything harder.

It is going to ask you to take it tomorrow, too.

And the day after that.

The argument of this book — the one I will spend the next eleven chapters making — is that what you are missing, in the season you are in, is not vision. It is not motivation. It is not, despite what the wellness influencers will sell you, mindset. What you are missing is an engine. You have lost the structure that gave your forward motion its momentum, and what you are calling stuckness is really just the absence of an engine where one used to be.

This book is going to give you a new one. Not the one you used to have. The structure that defined the last twenty years of your life — your job, your role, your team, your reason for getting up at 5:47 a.m. on a Wednesday — is over. You are right about that. Don't waste another year arguing with the obvious.

But the engine that ran underneath the structure?

That is still yours.

Here is what I mean by an engine.

When Renee was the CMO, she got out of bed at 5:47 a.m. on Wednesdays not because her body wanted to and not because she felt particularly inspired by Q3 brand-attribution metrics. She got out of bed because forty-three people on her team would be looking at her face at 9:30, and the call she had to take with the agency at 11 had been on the calendar for two weeks, and her boss was going to ask her about the new product launch on Thursday, and her oldest was applying to colleges and had asked her to read the essay before she left for work.

The engine that got her out of bed was not motivation. The engine was *obligation*.

Every adult who has ever moved forward through a hard season has run on the same engine. You do not get out of bed because you feel ready. You get out of bed because someone is counting on you. You make the call you do not want to make because the person on the other end needs you to. You write the next page of the dissertation because the version of you who started it three years ago does not deserve to be abandoned by the version of you who is tired tonight.

You show up at the hospital on Tuesday night because no one else is going to.

What you have lost, in this season of your life, is not your inspiration.

What you have lost is your sense of who is counting on you.

This book is going to help you find that again.

It is going to do it with three questions, which, in the chapters ahead, become three channels of forward motion you will run in parallel:

Who is your work for now?

What are you willing to build for the people around you?

Who is the person you are becoming, and what does that person need from you this week?

These three questions are not a personality test. They are not a values exercise. They are the three places your obligation lives. If you can find a credible answer in each, you have an engine. If you cannot find one yet, that is where the next right step belongs.

There is a sentence I am going to repeat enough times in this book that you will begin to see it before you turn the page:

The uniform changes. The duty doesn't.

The uniform you wore for the last twenty years is in the drawer. You don't get to put it back on. That is the part you are right to mourn, and this book will not insult you by pretending you should be over it. But underneath the uniform, under the title and the badge and the company email and the role you played at the dinner table, there was a duty. There was a reason you wore that uniform that was not, finally, the uniform itself.

That duty did not retire when the role did.

The work of this book is to find that duty, name it, and put on the next uniform. You will be slow to recognize the next uniform at first because it does not look much like the old one. The next uniform is rarely glamorous. It rarely fits the way the old one fit. It rarely earns you the kind of recognition you are used to. But it is, if you can bear with the awkwardness of putting it on, the way you keep going.

Renee, by the way, will be back. So will David, who made partner at his firm and cried in a parking garage on a Tuesday. And Mark, who took the early retirement package and is now eight months into a project I am going to ask you not to attempt. And Tom, who was a firefighter for thirty-one years and is currently teaching a free CPR class at the public library on Sunday mornings and has not been this happy in a decade. And John, who is recently widowed and learning, slowly, what it looks like to take one walk, one shower, one phone call. They are composites. The details have been changed. The situations are, in the country we live in right now, ordinary.

You will recognize them. Some of them are you.

The first job of the next eleven chapters is to make sure you can see yourself in this book and to give you something to do, in your actual life, by the end of every chapter you read.

A few things to say about how this book is built, before we go any further.

The book is not long. It is twelve chapters and a short closing coda. You can read it in three sittings if you want, or one chapter a week for the next twelve weeks if that is easier on the nervous system. I would recommend reading it through once, quickly, to get the shape of the argument. Then keep it by the bed and reread one chapter at a time, in order, the second time through. The chapters are designed to land harder the second time, when the part of you that resists has already had its first round of quiet objections.

Each chapter has a short reflection exercise at the end. The exercises are short on purpose. They are not journaling prompts in disguise. They are not designed to make you feel something. They are designed to give you something specific to do, today or this week, that you will not have to redo later. You can skip them. You can also do them. The book's argument does not require you to do them, but the book's results do.

I will, throughout, refer to people by name: Renee, David, Mark, Carla, Priya, Ramona, Tom, Aisha, John. Their stories are real in the way composites are real: anonymized, condensed, sometimes braided from more than one person. The details are accurate to what actually happened to actual people in transitions like the one you are in. I will also, occasionally, refer to my own life: the squadron I served in, the company I worked for after, the lacrosse league I started in my forties, the doctorate I went back for in my late forties. I am not the hero of this book. You are. I am the one who learned a few things on the way out of the room you are currently sitting in, and I am going to share them, plainly, for as long as it takes you to find your way to the next room.

I am not promising you transformation.

I am promising you that you will move.

If you read this book the way I am asking you to read it — once through, then a chapter at a time, with the small actions taken honestly — you will not be a different person on the back cover. You will be the same person, in motion. That is more than enough.

Take a sip of your coffee. It is getting cold.

Turn the page.

Chapter 1 — The Uniform You Didn't Know You Were Wearing

The first morning is the one you don't expect.

I woke up at 5:34 a.m. on a Tuesday in Jacksonville, in a house I owned, in a city I had chosen rather than been ordered to. There was no alarm. There hadn't been an alarm in years; the body wakes when it's ready, and it had been wired for nearly 20 years to be ready by 5:30. That part hadn't changed. The part that had changed was what I did next.

For a few seconds, it was a normal morning. Then I remembered there was no brief at 7. There was no flight schedule. There was no ready room I needed to walk into, no maintenance update I needed to get from the chief, and no one expecting me to be anywhere by any specific time in the next twelve hours.

And I stayed in bed longer than I should have.

That was the strange part. Not that I had time. That I felt vaguely like I was skipping something. Like, there was a thing I was supposed to be doing, and I was not doing it, and the absence of the thing was itself the wrongness. There wasn't anything to skip. The brief had ended, in a sense, two months ago, when I took off the uniform for the last time, and the Marine Corps stopped having anywhere it needed me to be. But the body had not received the memo.

The body was still in formation.

There were no orders waiting. There was no next move already decided. Just stay. That was new.

I got up eventually. I made coffee. I stood at the kitchen counter and held the cup for longer than the cup required, because there was no clock I was trying to beat. It should have felt like freedom. People had been telling me for months that it would feel like freedom. *You're going to love it,* they said. *You'll finally have time. You earned it.*

What it actually felt like was quiet in a way that was not yet comfortable.

I was not wearing anything that meant anything. That had never been true before. For 20 years, I had put on clothes every morning that told the world who I was before I said a word. The uniform did the talking. The uniform set the room. The uniform answered the question — even from strangers, even from store clerks, even from kids — *who is this guy and what is he supposed to be doing here?*

Now I was a man in normal clothes, standing in a kitchen, in a city I had chosen, holding a coffee cup, with nowhere to be.

That was the first morning. Nothing happened. That was what was wrong.

———————————————

Here is what I have come to understand about that morning, and about the months that followed it:

I was not in a midlife crisis. I was not in burnout. I was not depressed, or grieving, or having any of the things that twenty-first-century vocabulary has prepared me to name. I was something quieter and much harder to describe in a single word, which is part of why almost no one talks about it honestly.

I had taken off a uniform I did not know I had been wearing.

I knew about the literal uniform. The flight suit, the boots, the rank. I had taken those off ceremonially, with witnesses, with handshakes, with a small framed shadow box that now sits on a shelf in my office. That uniform was easy to take off because I knew it was a uniform.

The other uniform — the one this book is about — I did not know was a uniform until it was gone.

It was the structure of who I served. It was the cadence of what I owed and to whom. It was the assumption, baked so deeply into how I moved through a day that I had stopped noticing it, that I existed inside a system of obligations that gave my mornings their shape and my evenings their weight. The uniform was not the cloth. The uniform was the duty.

When the cloth came off, I expected to miss the cloth. What I missed, and could not name for a long time, was the thing the cloth had been holding in place.

That is the chapter you are reading. That is the first thing you have to name in order to move.

The first three months were not dramatic. I want to make sure that's clear, because the books in the next aisle of the store will tell you that the day after the role ends, you fall apart. You don't, mostly. The bills get paid. The lawn gets mowed. The kids ask what's for dinner, and dinner gets made. The world keeps moving, and you, technically, keep moving with it.

What you don't do — what nobody warns you about — is keep moving in the way that used to feel like *yours*.

I remember the first time the question landed in a way that pulled me up short. I was at a hardware store. I was looking at hose attachments, of all things. A guy a few feet away was looking at the same shelf, and we exchanged the small-talk nod that men exchange when they are pretending to know what they are doing in a hardware store, and he made one of those flat, friendly comments — *what do you do?* — the kind of question that fills the silence between strangers and means absolutely nothing.

For twenty years, that question had been the easiest question in the language.

Marine. Pilot.

Two words. Both true. Both, in a way I had never had cause to examine, did all the work for me. The question wasn't about my job. The question was about my place — in a country, in a culture, in a stranger's quick mental ranking of who I might be. Two words handled it.

That morning, in the hardware store, I hesitated.

I said, "I work for Boeing." Which was, by every measurable definition, true. I had a badge that worked. I had a salary that hit the account on the first and the fifteenth. I had a desk, meetings on the calendar, and a manager whose Outlook invitations I accepted without reading. *I work for Boeing* was the correct answer to the question the man had actually asked.

It just was not the answer I believed.

It felt like I had handed the man a job description instead of an introduction. The two words I had used for twenty years had not been a job description. They had been a *self*. And the self was no longer available, and the job description was what was left, and standing in front of a wall of brass hose fittings on a Tuesday afternoon, I noticed for the first time what a thin substitute one is for the other.

That gap — between what was true and what felt true — is the chapter I am now writing.

I want to say more about the months that followed, because I think they will sound familiar even if your particulars are nothing like mine.

I kept waking up at 5:30. The body did not stop. For two years, the body did not stop. There was a stretch where I tried to sleep in on Saturdays, and the body still got me up at 5:30, and I lay there in the dark trying to remember what I had done with that hour for the last twenty years, and what I was supposed to do with it now.

I caught myself scanning rooms. Walking into a restaurant, into a meeting, into a child's birthday party — my eyes were doing what my eyes had been trained to do for years. *Who's in charge here? Who's tracking? Who's not paying attention? Where's the door?* I did not consciously think any of this. I had stopped consciously thinking it years before, the way a long-married couple stops consciously checking that the other one is still in the room. The body kept doing it. The trained reflex didn't know the training was over.

I would notice how people carried themselves. Who was squared away. Who was not. I want to be careful here. This is not a brag, and it is not a judgment of the people I was looking at. It is a description of what twenty years of training does to your perception. You can take the boots off. You cannot take the perception off. Not in the first three months. Not in the first three years.

There were moments — small, internal moments — when I almost introduced myself differently than I should have. Not out loud. You can feel an introduction forming before you make it, the way you can feel a sneeze. *Captain. Major.* Two-word answers were coming up that I had to swallow before I said them. The right two words were no longer my words. The body had an old answer ready, and the mind had a new answer it was still practicing, and for several months, the old one was faster.

There was a particular way I carried time. In the squadron, time had cost. You did not waste it. You moved with purpose. Hours had a hardness to them, and tasks had edges, and the day was a thing you advanced through, deliberately, not a thing you sat inside. Civilian time moves differently. It is softer. It bends around late-starting meetings. It accommodates people deciding what they want to do over lunch. For the first few months, I felt the speed of the world around me as a kind of friction. Not slower, exactly. Less directional. The day did not advance toward anything in particular, and I had to learn how to live in a time without a beginning or an end.

There was a particular sense — and this is the one that, to me, captures the period most exactly — that I should be preparing for something. The body still felt the proximity of something coming. A briefing. A formation. A flight. An order. *Be ready.* That had been the underlying note of twenty years of mornings, and the note did not stop just because there was now no music.

Except there wasn't anything specific anymore.

I would walk through a Tuesday with the residual ready-for-something running quietly underneath everything I did, and there would be no thing for the readiness to be for. The readiness had no object. The readiness was a phantom limb.

That is what the first three months were. Not dramatic. Not collapse. A man in normal clothes, in a chosen city, with a job that paid well, holding the residue of a self that no longer had a context. At 5:34 a.m., standing at the kitchen counter, longer than the cup required.

There was something I was not saying to anyone at the time. I will say it here, because the rest of this book will not work if I don't.

I was not saying how much of my identity had been tied to what I had been doing. I was not saying that some days I quietly wondered whether the most meaningful work I would ever do in my life was already behind me. I was not saying that I did not yet know how to replace the sense of purpose I had lost — not just the professional purpose, but the deeper one, the one that had given Tuesday afternoons their weight. I was not saying that the uncertainty was bothering me more than I had expected.

To everyone who knew me from the outside, things looked fine. Good job. Stable life. Forward momentum.

What it actually felt like, on the inside, was recalibrating without a clear reference point.

I tell you this not because I want sympathy, but because the version of you reading this book right now is most likely also not saying something, and the not-saying is part of the cavity. You can move forward without telling anyone what you are not saying. But the book is not going to be useful to you if you don't, at minimum, admit it to yourself.

If I am the example that comes first, Renee is the example that proves it is not just a military thing.

I want to come back to her, because by now you have met her — the kitchen, the mug, the nineteen days. There is a detail about her that I did not include in the introduction because it would have been too much too early in the book, but it belongs in this chapter.

She kept drafting messages to her team.

Not on her phone. She had been removed from the company Slack on day two, and her work email had been deactivated by the morning of day three. The technology had moved more quickly than her body had. The technology had handled the role-change cleanly. The body did not know the role had changed.

So she drafted the messages in her head.

She would notice something in the news that touched a campaign her team had been running. Her brain would, in the background, compose a Slack message. *Hey team, just saw this — let's talk Monday about whether we want to nudge the language in the new spot.* She would have the message half-written before she remembered there was no team. There was no Slack. There was no Monday meeting. The compose box was a phantom, the same way my readiness for a brief was a phantom, the same way my eyes scanning a restaurant were a phantom.

The body and the brain had been wearing a uniform for the last twelve years that nobody, including Renee, had been calling a uniform.

She thought she had a job. She did. She also had a uniform. The uniform was not the title on her business card. The uniform was the structure of being someone people brought problems to — at 9:30, at 11, at 2, at 4, at 5:55 just before she logged off. Forty-three people on her team had problems. The problems came to her. She solved them, escalated them, or taught the team how to solve them next time. Twelve years of solving problems had wired Renee's body to expect problems. When the problems stopped, the body did not.

For about three weeks, she kept catching herself reaching for the laptop in the way I kept catching myself getting up at 5:30. The body has a memory, and the memory does not respect resignation letters.

I want you to notice how plain Renee's situation is.

She is not, in any sense that would make the news, in trouble. Her health is fine. Her marriage is fine. Her finances are, as of nineteen days into this, more than fine. Anyone looking at her life from the outside would say she is, in their language, *transitioning*. And she is. But the language flattens what is actually happening. What is actually happening is that a uniform she did not know was a uniform has been removed from her body, and her body is still trying to perform inside it, and she has begun to suspect that what she is grieving is not the role but the *self the role was holding in place.*

That is the chapter you are reading.

If your uniform were a flight suit, you might recognize this faster than someone whose uniform was a CMO badge. But the structure is the same. The duty is the same. The fact that the body kept moving as though the duty were still in force is the same.

You are not in a job transition. You are in a uniform transition.

That is a different problem, and it requires a different first move.

Here is the argument of this chapter, and it will sit underneath everything that comes next:

You do not grieve a job. You grieve a self.

When the role you played for ten or twenty or thirty years ends, the language that arrives to help you is the language of *career*. Severance. Transition. Pivot. Next chapter. The internet's algorithm, sensing the change, will start serving you ads for résumé reviewers and second-act coaches. Your brother-in-law will tell you about a friend of a friend who took a year off and then started a consulting practice. Everyone will assume what you have lost is *work*.

What you have lost is a self.

Not the whole self. You are still here. You still know your kids' middle names. You still remember how to drive home from the grocery store. You are not, in the dramatic sense the language wants you to be, *gone.* But a piece of who you understood yourself to be — a piece you may not have known was inside the role — has come out with the role, and the cavity it left is what you are walking around with now.

Most stuckness in midlife is the sensation of that cavity.

Most cases of stuckness in midlife get misdiagnosed because the cavity is invisible. You can't show it to your wife. You can't show it to your therapist. You can't show it to the friend who keeps sending you links to entrepreneurship podcasts. The cavity is not in your résumé. It is not in your finances. It is not in any conversation where someone asks you about your *plans*. The cavity is in the place where you used to know, without thinking about it, what you were for.

Naming the uniform is the first move because it makes the cavity visible.

You cannot grieve what you have not named. You cannot replace what you have not grieved. You cannot move toward something next when you have not yet acknowledged that what you actually lost is not a job but a *part of who you were inside the job.*

Most readers of this book have been told, by well-meaning people in their lives, that they are being too hard on themselves. *It was just a job. Lots of people leave companies. You'll find something else.* The well-meaning people are wrong. Not about you finding something else; you probably will. They are wrong about the size of what you are dealing with. It was not just a job. It was a structure inside which a self took shape. The structure is gone. The self is now, for a while, on its own.

This is not a dignified state. It is not pretty. The books in the next aisle of the store, the ones with bright covers and big bold titles about reinvention, will not tell you that. They will tell you, more or less, that the next chapter is going to be *better*. That you are about to *unlock* something. That your best years are ahead. Maybe they are. I am not here to argue with that.

What I am here to tell you is that there is a chapter before that chapter, and it is the chapter you are in right now, and you cannot skip it. You can pretend to skip it. You can fill the next eight months with productive-looking activity and tell everyone at Thanksgiving that you are *exploring*. The cavity will still be there. It will follow you into the new project. It will follow you into the new company. It will follow you into the next year, and the year after that, until the day you finally sit at a kitchen counter and admit, to no one but yourself, that the uniform you took off was not the uniform you thought it was.

Naming it is the move.

The rest of the book is about what to do once you have.

You may be raising one of three objections in your head right now, and I want to answer all three before we go further. If I don't, you will spend the next eleven chapters arguing with the book in your head instead of reading it.

The first objection is: *But I chose to leave.* I retired voluntarily. I took the package. I had been planning the exit for a year. I am not the laid-off CMO; this is not happening to me, this is something I am doing.

I hear you. Choosing to take the uniform off does not mean you understood what was inside it. The uniform doesn't care whether you left it or it left you. The cavity is the same cavity. The only difference is that, because you chose, you may feel less entitled to the grief. Some of the readers of this book who chose are having a harder time than the readers who didn't, because they have been telling themselves, for a year of planning and three months of execution, that this was *what they wanted.* It was. And it is also costing them more than they expected. Both can be true.

The second objection is: *I'm grateful. I had a great run. I have nothing to complain about.* You are right. You did, you do, and you don't. None of those facts changes the cavity. You can be grateful for a uniform and still grieve its removal. Gratitude does not preempt grief; gratitude that pretends to is just denial in nicer clothing.

The third objection is: *I'm too old to be having an identity crisis.* This is the one I want to push back on hardest, because it is the one most readers of this book are quietly carrying. There is a story in the culture that says identity questions belong to people in their twenties. Twenty-year-olds are *finding themselves.* Forty-year-olds are supposed to *have themselves.* The math is simple, and it is wrong. The math assumes that the self is something you find once and then keep, like a wallet or a passport. In practice, the self takes shape within the structures you live in, and when those structures end, the self has to take a new shape. People in their fifties have this. People in their seventies have it. People who are dying have it. The notion that this is something one outgrows is a cultural superstition. It has the unfortunate effect of making the readers who experience it past forty feel embarrassed about it, which means they don't talk about it, which means they don't get help with it, which is why a great many of them are reading a book like this in the first place. Don't be embarrassed. Be honest. Honesty is the move.

The first practical move in this book is small and not glamorous, which will be a theme.

It is called the uniform inventory.

Take a piece of paper, or open a fresh document on your laptop, or — if you are the kind of person who does this best by hand on the back of an envelope at 11 p.m. — do that. The medium does not matter. What matters is that the inventory exists in some form you can come back to, because we will refer to it three more times in this book.

For each uniform you have worn — literal or figurative — write down four things.

The years you wore it. (When did it start. When did it end? If it has not ended yet, leave the second date blank.)

What it was. (Be plain. *Marine officer. Stay-at-home mom. Senior engineer at a Fortune 500. Pastor of a 600-person congregation. Founder and CEO of a startup that sold to a competitor in 2022.*)

Who did you serve in it? (The team. The flock. The kids. The customers. The community. Be specific where you can.)

What did it teach you? (One sentence. Not a paragraph. The thing the uniform turned out, when you got far enough from it to see, to have been *for*.)

Most readers, when they do this honestly, find they have worn three or four uniforms — sometimes more — that they had not been counting as uniforms. The athlete who became a coach. The parent of small children who became the parent of teenagers. The associate who became a partner. The engineer who became a manager. Each of those was a different uniform. Each, in its own way, came off.

The inventory is not for the book. It is for you. You do not have to share it with anyone. You should, in fact, share it with no one until you have lived with it for a week. The temptation to show your spouse, or post a sanitized version on LinkedIn, will be strong. Resist it. The inventory is meant to be looked at by you, alone, until it has been honest for long enough to be useful.

When you are done, stay with the list for a while. Notice which uniform was the longest. Notice which one was the heaviest. Notice which one is the one whose absence, if you are being honest, you are still carrying.

That last one is the chapter you are in.

We will end every chapter the same way: with a short, specific reflection. The reflections are bounded, usually by word count, sometimes by time. They are not designed to make you feel something. They are designed to give you something specific to do today or this week that won't need to be redone later.

Here is the reflection for this chapter:

Write three sentences describing the uniform you wore the longest. Be physical: what you put on, what you carried, who you served, what others called you. Do not write more than three sentences. Two hundred words, maximum. The constraint matters.

You will be tempted to write more. Don't. The point of the constraint is to force you to choose what was *most* true about the uniform, not to comprehensively describe it. There is a different uniform inventory you have already completed — on the back of an envelope or in a new document — that contains the rest. This sentence-level reflection is the headline. The most true sentence about the most significant uniform you wore.

Save the three sentences. We will come back to them.

A note before we close this chapter and go on to the next.

You have just done — or you will do, in the next day or two, when the moment is right — the most important first move in this book. You have named the uniform you did not know you were wearing. The cavity that has been following you around for weeks, months, or years now has a shape and a location. It is no longer the unspecified weight in the chest that woke you up at 3 a.m. last Thursday. It has a name. It is the absence of a specific thing. That alone is a relief, and it's worth sitting with for a day or two before you push on.

When you are ready, the next question is the one almost no one in your life is going to ask you out loud, and the one you are most quietly afraid to answer:

If everything in my life is technically fine, why does the room still feel empty?

That is Chapter 2.

Chapter 2 — Why You Look Successful and Feel Stuck

David made partner on a Thursday in May.

It was the youngest-partner-ever announcement at the firm — the kind of internal news that gets announced in a partner's meeting, then spreads to the associates by 2 p.m., then sits in the firm's external press release the following Monday. There were calls from the headhunters who had been circling him for years. There was a congratulatory note from the managing partner, written by hand on the firm's heavy ivory stock. There was a dinner, three weeks later, at the steakhouse the firm used for things like this — speeches at the dessert course, two of the senior partners walking to the microphone with their reading glasses, the kind of remarks that everyone at the table has heard before but pretends not to have. David's wife wore the dress she had been saving for occasions like this. His mother flew up from Atlanta and cried during the speeches.

And then everyone went home.

David drove. His wife had had two glasses of wine and was saying something about whether they should finally renovate the kitchen, now that they could. He was nodding. The car was a four-year-old Audi he had been meaning to replace and now would. The radio was on low — some piece of jazz, which was the genre his wife liked at the end of a long evening, which David could take or leave but had grown used to over twenty-three years of marriage.

About six minutes into the drive, he turned the radio off.

He did not say why. He was not aware, really, that he had done it. His wife noticed and asked if everything was all right and he said yes, fine, just tired. They drove the rest of the way in a silence that was, by the standards of their marriage, ordinary. She did not press. He was grateful that she did not press.

What he did not say was that the silence was less unbearable than the noise. That the music had been doing something to him in the car that he had not yet found a word for. That he had been thinking, while the saxophone played and his wife talked about kitchen counters, *this was the thing.*

This was the thing he had been working toward for fifteen years.

He had been made a partner at a top firm. Younger than anyone in the firm's history. There were two hundred attorneys in the office, every one of them on some version of the same path he had been on, and he was now ahead of all of them. The dinner was over. The speeches had been said. The dress would go back into the closet and the mother would fly back to Atlanta and the headhunter calls would taper off in a week or two, and tomorrow, Friday, he would walk into the office at 7:15 the way he always did, and he would do the work he had always done, with one extra word now after his name on the firm directory.

And he had absolutely no idea what to do with the rest of his life.

He could not tell his wife. He could not tell his mother. He could not tell the colleagues whose names he had collected on the cards from the steakhouse table. He could not tell his oldest friend from law school, who had texted *holy shit, you did it* at 4:47 that afternoon. The thing he was thinking was the kind of thing you could not say out loud at the dinner the firm had thrown to celebrate you.

The thing he was thinking was: *this was the destination. I am here. The view is fine. I'm unclear on what the next ten years are supposed to be for.*

That was on a Thursday in May.

By the following Tuesday in July, he was crying in the parking garage of the firm's office tower, hiding behind a concrete pillar so the cleaning crew wouldn't see him. He could not tell his wife about that either.

———————————

Here is what David was running into, and what a great many readers of this book are also running into and have not yet named:

His external life and his internal direction had decoupled.

For fifteen years, the two had been welded together. The thing he was supposed to do — the thing the firm wanted him to do, the thing his family expected him to do, the thing the larger story he was inside of had named as *forward* — was the same thing he was internally moving toward. *Make partner.* When you have a clear external goal that is also your internal goal, the question of forward motion does not arise. You don't ask whether you are moving forward. The world is telling you, in a thousand small ways, that you are.

When the external goal is reached, that machinery stops.

It does not stop quietly. The world keeps trying to feed you forward motion: *now you should be working toward equity partner, now you should be acquiring book of business, now you should be sitting on boards.* The signals keep coming. The signals are no longer aligned with anything inside you. Your body keeps moving, but the direction is no longer yours. It is the direction the system happens to be pointing at, because the system never stops pointing.

This is the gap David hit in the parking garage.

It was not a failure. It was an achievement, at the same time, a void in direction. The two are not opposites. They are the most common pair in the lives of the readers of this book.

The chapter you are reading is about how to name that gap so it stops eating you alive.

———————————

I want to tell you what happened to David in the parking garage because the specifics are useful and will probably remind you of a moment of your own.

Tuesday in July was unremarkable. He had been at the office since 7:15, the way he always was. He had taken three calls that morning, one of them from a senior client whose company was being acquired and who needed legal cover for a board move that was, in David's professional opinion, a bad idea executed by an arrogant CEO. He had eaten a salad at his desk for lunch. He had reviewed a brief his second-year associate had drafted, which was a mediocre brief that he had to mostly rewrite, which was the kind of work he had done thousands of times and would do thousands more times before he retired, and which on this particular Tuesday felt, for the first time, *small*.

The smallness was the new problem. The work had not gotten smaller. He had outgrown the expectation that the work was the thing.

He left the office at 6:30. He took the elevator down to the parking garage. He walked the two and a half levels to where his Audi was parked — the same Audi he had been about to replace in May and had not gotten around to replacing because, he now noticed, he didn't actually care what kind of car he was driving. He sat in the driver's seat. He put his hands on the steering wheel. And without any particular warning, the way these things happen to forty-eight-year-old men who have been holding something in for ten weeks, he started crying.

It was not a small cry. It was the kind of cry that is fifteen years late.

He cried, by his later estimate, for about eleven minutes. He hid the worst of it behind a concrete pillar he had pulled the car next to, though there was no one in the garage at 6:32 in the evening except the cleaning crew on the level below. He cried because he had made partner and the world had not, finally, gotten any larger. He cried because he was forty-eight and could not fully tell his wife what was wrong, because he could not say *I am unhappy at the top* without sounding either entitled or insane. He cried because he had spent fifteen years working toward a specific external thing, had hit it cleanly, and had discovered, on the other side of the hit, that the thing did not contain what he had assumed it contained.

He had assumed the thing would contain a *next direction.* Most of us assume this about most of the things we work toward.

It did not.

When he finished crying, he wiped his face with a napkin from a McDonald's bag in the passenger seat. He drove home. He told his wife he had had a long day. He ate the dinner she had made. He played catch with his eleven-year-old in the driveway for twenty minutes. He went to bed at 10:30. He woke up the next morning at 5:45 and went to work, and made partnership-level decisions, and ate a salad at his desk, and the world continued to point at things he had once been moving toward and was no longer moving toward, because there was no longer a thing inside him doing the pointing.

This is what most stuckness in midlife actually looks like.

It does not look like a collapse. It looks like a man in a very nice car, at the top of a profession, hiding from the cleaning crew behind a parking-garage pillar at 6:32 on a Tuesday, crying because the destination was not the destination he had been told it would be.

It looks like a woman in a kitchen in a robe she has worn for fifteen years, holding a mug that says CHIEF MARKETING OFFICER, nineteen days into the silence after the role ended.

It looks like a man at a kitchen counter in Jacksonville, holding a coffee cup longer than it should have, on a Tuesday morning when the body still wanted to be in formation.

It looks like a woman who founded a non-profit fifteen years ago, sitting alone at the office on a Sunday afternoon after the board has agreed to the succession plan, looking at her name on the door and realizing she has not, until this moment, asked herself what she will do when the door has someone else's name on it.

It looks like a man whose youngest child just left for college, walking into a daughter's empty bedroom on a Wednesday in late August, sitting on the unmade bed, and noticing that he has not had a thing to do with his hands at 7 p.m. on a Wednesday in twenty-two years.

It looks like a woman who sold her company in March and was supposed to be on a sailboat in May and is, instead, in a Whole Foods at 2 p.m. on a Tuesday, looking at the rotisserie chickens, not because she wants a rotisserie chicken but because she does not have anywhere else to be.

The shape is the same. The uniforms are different. What is missing is the same thing.

You hit what you were supposed to hit. You arrived where you were supposed to arrive. And you noticed, perhaps for the first time, that the *arrival* had been doing all the work of giving your life its shape, that the arrival was now behind you, and that the people around you were still operating as though the arrival was the point.

You can get a lot of help with the climb. There are books, mentors, coaches, podcasts, half the internet, your in-laws, your parents, the fitness industry, the productivity industry — all of them are organized around the climb. There is a much smaller and quieter set of voices that will help you with what comes after.

This book is going to be one of them.

———————————————

I had a quieter version of David's parking garage.

I want to be careful to say: I did not cry in any parking garage. The version of this I lived through was quieter, longer, and probably more familiar to most readers of this book than David's, because most stuckness is quieter than the dinner-and-speeches kind. Most people don't get a partnership announcement. Most people don't get a moment when the firm sends out a press release. Most people get a Tuesday at a desk on which they realized, by themselves, that something was off.

That is what my Boeing years were.

I would walk into the building in the morning. I had a badge that worked. I had a salary that hit the account on the first and the fifteenth. I had meetings on the calendar with people whose work mattered to a mission I still believed in, in a way that was real, even if it was different from the way it had been real in a flight suit. I would sit in those meetings and say things that were useful and contributed to decisions that affected systems that would eventually make the warfighter's life better in ways I cared about.

There were Tuesday afternoons in Boeing conference rooms when I would catch myself noticing how different the texture of the work was from what I had been used to. Not better, not worse. Different. The work I had done in a flight suit had an *immediacy* that the work I was doing now lacked. The mission still mattered. The loop between effort and consequence was just longer, quieter, and harder to feel. I am not making a value claim. I am making a structural one. The shape of the work was different, and the shape was doing something to me that I had not yet named.

And inside, underneath all of that, was a question that would not go away.

The question was not *am I unhappy.* I was not unhappy. The question was not *should I leave.* I was not, on most days, thinking about leaving. The question — and I want to be precise about this, because I think the precision will help you — was something more like: *is this the shape my mission is supposed to take now?** I had a job. I was not asking whether I had a job. I was asking whether the job was the *self.*

The two are not the same question.

A great many people on this side of forty, who from the outside look exactly like they should be content, are quietly carrying that question. They are not unhappy. They are not in trouble. They are not, by any external measure, doing anything wrong. They have a question they cannot fully ask out loud — sometimes not even to themselves — about whether the structure they are inside is still, fully, the structure their *self* belongs in. The question is not loud. The question is not constant. But it is present enough, on enough Tuesdays at enough desks, that the people carrying it have begun to suspect they are not getting away with something.

That was my Boeing era, just as David's parking garage was his.

The texture of it was different. The volume was different. The privacy of it was different. The structure was identical.

The reason I am putting these two stories side by side is that I want you to see how plainly the same shape shows up in different lives. David's life looked like a partnership track and a steakhouse dinner. Mine looked like a defense contractor's badge and a Tuesday in a beige conference room. The reader I am writing this book for has their own version. The version is not the point. The shape is the point.

The shape is *successful from the outside. Hollow from the inside. And not entitled to mention it.*

Let me say what is happening, mechanically, in lives like David's, Renee's, mine, and yours.

The first thirty-some years of an adult life are typically organized around a *climb*. The climb is named differently depending on whose life it is. *Get the degree. Make the rank. Make the partner. Build the company. Make a marriage. Raise the kids until they are people. Pay off the mortgage. Get the title with the corner office.* The specific climb varies. The structure of the climb is the same: you are pointed at a destination that is genuinely difficult, that takes years, that is recognized by the people around you as a worthy thing to be pointed at, and that requires you to make daily small efforts that, over decades, deliver you to the top.

The climb is the easy part.

I know it does not feel like the easy part while you are doing it. The work of the climb is real. The hours are real. The losses on the way up — the marriages strained, the kids you missed, the friends who fell off, the years you do not get back — those are real too. I am not minimizing the climb. I am saying that *the climb is structurally simple.* You know where you are going. You know what counts. You know what doesn't. The signals from the world around you are aligned with your internal direction. You move forward, and the world tells you that you are, in fact, moving forward.

What no one warns you about is what happens at the top.

At the top, the signals do not stop. The world is still telling you that you are moving forward. The world has more rungs ready for you. *Equity partner. Senior managing director. EVP. Board seat.* The next rung is always available. What changes, if you are paying attention — and most people on this side of forty are paying attention, even if they don't have the language for it yet — is that the next rung is no longer where your internal direction is pointing.

The internal direction has gone quiet.

It has gone quiet because the work of the climb did not require you to develop a *direction* of your own. The climb came with one. *Up.* That was sufficient. While you were climbing, the question of *what direction is mine* was answered by the climb itself; you didn't have to ask it. Now the climb is over. There is no internal answer ready, because there has not been an internal answer needed for thirty years. The system is asking you to keep moving. Your internal compass has not yet been built for the place you are now standing.

That is the gap.

The gap is the cavity from Chapter 1, looked at from a different angle. Chapter 1 named what came off — the uniform, the structure, the duty-as-shape. Chapter 2 names what was *underneath* the uniform that you did not have to develop because the uniform was doing it for you: a sense of where you were going on your own.

Most readers of this book do not have that sense. Not because they are lazy or shallow or insufficiently introspective. Because they have spent thirty years inside a structure that did the directional work *for* them, and the structure was so well-designed and so widely endorsed that it never occurred to them to ask whether the destination it was pointing them at was, finally, theirs.

It probably was, mostly. That is not the question. The question is whether what comes *after* the destination is theirs.

That is what the next ten chapters are about. But before we go there, we have to sit, for a chapter, with the discomfort of having reached a place we worked thirty years to reach and discovering that we don't yet know what to do with our hands.

Three objections will come to mind as you read this, and I want to answer them now.

The first objection is: *but other people have it worse.* People are losing jobs. People are losing houses. People are sick. People are alone. Who am I to be sitting in a parking garage feeling stuck when I just made partner? Who am I to be wondering about the shape of my mission when there are people across town who are wondering about rent?

The objection has two parts. The first part — *yes, other people have it worse* — is true. The second part — *therefore I have no right to feel what I am feeling* — is false. Suffering is not a competition. There is no leaderboard on which your discomfort is canceled by someone else's worse discomfort. The person across town with the rent problem is also entitled to their own difficulty, and so are you. The fact that your difficulty is invisible does not make it not a difficulty. It just makes it invisible.

The second objection is: *I have nothing to complain about.* You are not complaining. You are noticing. There is a difference. Complaining is a posture; it asks the world to fix something. Noticing is a posture; it asks you to *see* something. The chapter is asking you to notice, not complain. The complaint, if you let it form, would be the wrong move. The notice is the move.

The third objection is: *this is just a failure of gratitude.* You should be grateful. You should appreciate what you have. You should count your blessings. You should —, and this is the favorite verb of every well-meaning person who has ever told you to be grateful — *put it in perspective.*

I want to be careful here, because I am not telling you to abandon gratitude. Gratitude is real, and I owe a great deal of mine to people I will not adequately thank in my lifetime. Gratitude, when it is real, makes you more honest, not less. The version of gratitude that makes you less honest is *performed* gratitude — gratitude as a social signal, gratitude as a reason to stop noticing, gratitude as a way to skip the chapter you are in. That is not gratitude. That is denial wearing gratitude's clothing. The chapter is asking you to be honest, which is a precondition for the gratitude that is real, and which is incompatible with the gratitude that is theatrical.

You are not ungrateful. You are at a moment in your life when the gap between what you have and what you are pointed at has gotten too wide to ignore. That is the moment this book exists for.

The practice for this chapter is small, plain, and slightly uncomfortable. It is called honest accounting.

Take a single piece of paper. Draw a line down the middle.

On the left side, write *Already done.* Below it, list five things you have accomplished that the world would call success. Be plain. *Made partner. Raised three kids who are not in trouble. Paid off the house. Hit a million in revenue. Earned a Ph.D.* Whatever your version is. Five items, no more. The constraint matters; the choosing is the practice.

On the right side, write *Tomorrow.* Below it, list one thing you would have to do tomorrow to feel like you had moved.

Just one.

The point of the exercise is not to feel bad about how full the left side is or how empty the right side is. The point is to notice the gap. Most readers, when they do this honestly, find that the left side fills easily and the right side does not. That is the diagnosis. The left side has been receiving your attention for thirty years; of course, it is full. The right side has not been receiving your attention for thirty years; of course, it is hard.

A few rules.

The right-side item cannot be on the left side. *Make a bigger deal at work* is on the left side, even if you have not made it yet, because it is the same kind of thing. The right-side item has to be a different kind of thing. *Call my brother. Sit with my daughter and ask her what she thinks her life is about. Walk into the church I drive past every Sunday. Apply to the master's program I have been telling myself I am too old for the master's program. Open the file with the half-finished novel.* The right side is the place where the *next direction* lives, and the next direction is, almost by definition, not on the left side.

The right-side item also cannot be a *plan*. It has to be a thing you would have to do tomorrow. Not next month. Not after the kids are out of college. Not when the bonus comes in. Tomorrow.

You may find that the right-side item is hard to write. That is the point. The right side is hard to write because the left side has been doing all your forward motion for thirty years, and the muscle that does internal direction has atrophied. The honest accounting is the first rep.

Save the paper. We will come back to it.

The reflection for this chapter is the honest accounting itself, in its bounded form:

> *On a single piece of paper, draw a line down the middle. On the*
> *left, list five things you have accomplished that the world would*

call success. On the right, name one thing you would have to
do tomorrow to feel like you had moved. Five items on the left,
one on the right. No more. Notice which side was easier to fill.

You have one day to do it. (If you do not do it today, you will not do it.) When you have it, save it. We will come back to it three more times in this book.

———————————

A note before we go on.

You have just done the second naming move of the book. In Chapter 1, you named the uniform. In Chapter 2, you named the gap between the climb you completed and the direction that has not yet been shown. The gap is uncomfortable. I cannot make it less uncomfortable. What I can tell you is that the gap is not a sign that something is wrong with you. It is the *standard human response* to having reached a destination that was constructed by someone else and discovering, on the other side of it, that you are now in charge of a question you did not previously have to answer.

Sit with the gap. Do not rush past it. Do not fill it with productive activity in the next twenty-four hours, so you don't have to feel it. Do not tell your wife about it tonight. Do not post about it on LinkedIn. Do not research a new degree program at midnight. Let the gap be a gap for a day. The book will still be here tomorrow.

The next chapter is about the answer most readers reach for first.

It is the wrong answer.

If the standard prescription — *find your passion, follow what lights you up* — were going to work for you, it would have worked already. There is a reason it didn't, and that reason is more useful than the prescription.

That is Chapter 3.

Chapter 3 — The Lie You've Been Told About Passion

Mark took the early-retirement package on a Friday in September, eight months and two weeks ago.

He had told everyone — his wife, his three adult children, his brother in Phoenix, the friends at his retirement dinner, the people on LinkedIn who congratulated him on his "next chapter" — that he was finally going to figure out what he loved. He used those words. *Figure out what I love.* He had said the phrase enough times in the months leading up to the package that, by the time he actually took it, the phrase had calcified into a plan. There was a thing out there he loved. He was going to find it. He had thirty-two years of weekends back, a 401(k), his health, and a patient wife. He was going to do the thing the men at the retirement dinner kept telling him to do, which was to *take some time, listen to himself, see what called to him.*

It is now late May. Mark is in the garage, looking at the things he has bought.

There is a woodworking bench, $1,840, with a set of chisels he has used twice. There is a Sony camera with a lens kit, which has been to one weekend trip in February and has not been out of the bag since. There is a stack of cooking-class vouchers his wife gave him for Christmas, two of which have expired. There is a mountain bike, a fourteen-speed, $2,200 bike, which he rode three times and hated because, it turns out, his knees no longer want to do that. He bought a coffee-roasting setup after watching a YouTube video about the importance of sourcing your own beans. There is a guitar.

There is a guitar he has not touched.

In a notebook on the workbench — which Mark also bought, leather-bound, because he was going to journal — there are seven half-completed entries from the first month after his retirement, and then nothing. The most recent entry, written in November, ends mid-sentence with the words *I think the thing I actually*

He never finished the thought.

Mark is fifty-three years old. He took the package because he was supposed to be ready. He has done what a great many men in his position are told to do: cleared his calendar, opened his life, given himself permission to *follow what calls him.* Eight months in, what he has called him is approximately $11,400 worth of hobbies he no longer wants to look at, a bedroom upstairs that he has been avoiding because his wife asks gently in the morning what he is going to do today, and a quiet conviction that something is wrong with him.

There is nothing wrong with Mark. The advice was wrong.

This chapter is about the advice.

Here is what most readers of this book have been told, in many versions, by many well-meaning people:

Find your passion. Follow what lights you up. Listen to your inner voice. Discover what you were meant to do. Pursue your purpose. The thing you love is out there; you just need to find it.

I am going to ask you to set this advice down for the duration of this chapter, and possibly for the duration of the rest of your life.

The advice is wrong. Not partly wrong. Not wrong-with-exceptions. Wrong in the deep sense, which is that it assumes a thing about how you are built that is not true of you, or me, or Mark, or most of the readers of this book.

The advice assumes that *passion is something you find.*

The advice assumes that there is a thing — a calling, a purpose, a vocation, a hidden self — sitting somewhere in the world or in you, and that the work of the season after the climb is to *uncover* it. The advice assumes the work is detective work. The advice assumes that, if you are stuck at fifty-three with eight months of unused hobbies in a garage, you have not yet looked hard enough.

You have looked hard enough.

The advice does not work because the underlying model is wrong. Passion is not something you find. Passion is something you build, in the place where you are responsible to people you have decided to be responsible to, doing work that costs you something, over a long enough stretch of time that the doing eventually changes the doer.

You cannot find that. You can only do it.

That is the chapter you are reading.

Let me come back to Mark for a minute, because the texture of his eight months matters, and the texture is probably going to remind you of a stretch in your own life — either the one you are in now or the one you can feel approaching.

Mark did not start out aimless. The first week of his retirement was the best week. He slept in once, the way men who have been getting up at 5:30 for thirty years sleep in, which is to wake at 5:32 and lie in bed until 6:15, feeling decadent. He cooked his wife pancakes. He took a long walk on the beach. He went to a hardware store and walked around for two hours just because he could. *This is going to be great,* he said to his wife on Sunday night. *I have all this time. I'm going to figure out what I actually want.*

Week two, he started the lists.

The lists were not unreasonable. He had been told by enough podcasts, books, and well-meaning friends that the way to find your next thing was to brainstorm — to write down everything you were curious about, to circle the items that gave you energy, to follow the energy. He listed twenty-three items. *Photography. Woodworking. Mountain biking. Coffee. Guitar. Writing. Cooking. Mentoring younger guys. Volunteering at the church. Starting a small business. Sailing. Learning Spanish. Teaching. Travel. Reading more. Going back to school. Restoring an old car. Helping his oldest kid with her business plan. Coaching the high-school team. Getting fit again. Working with veterans. Building a treehouse for the grandkids. Finishing the novel he started in his thirties.* The lists were thorough. The lists were the work the advice had told him to do.

Week three, he started buying things.

This was not, in his mind, frivolity. The advice had also said that you have to *try things* — that you cannot know what calls to you until you do it, and you cannot do it without the basic equipment. The woodworking bench was bought to *try* woodworking. The camera was bought to *try* photography. The guitar was bought to *try* music. Each purchase was, in Mark's defense, the conscientious application of a method he had been told would work.

The method did not work.

By week eight, Mark had noticed something: the things on the list that gave him a small amount of energy when he listed them did not give him any energy at all when he tried them. The woodworking was tedious. The photography felt like Instagram preparation. The coffee roasting filled the kitchen with a smell his wife disliked. The guitar was harder than he had expected, and he did not, on most evenings, have the discipline to practice through the dull middle weeks where you are not yet good enough to enjoy what you are playing. None of it was *bad.* None of it was the thing.

By month three, he had started to suspect that the failure was his.

By month five, he had started to *believe* the failure was his.

The version of Mark in May, in the garage, looking at the bench, the camera, and the guitar, is not the version of Mark who took the package in September. The version in May has begun to organize the experience as a story about *himself.* He does not have what other people have. He is not capable of joy in retirement. He is the kind of man who burns through hobbies. Maybe the friends were right when they joked at the dinner that he wouldn't last a year without work. Maybe his wife is patient because she has accepted that this is who he is now. Maybe the most meaningful chapters of his life are behind him.

This is the place where the advice does its real damage.

The advice does not damage you when it fails to deliver passion. The advice damages you when the failure to deliver gets *internalized as a story about your character.* You did not fail to find a passion because something is wrong with you. You failed to find a passion because the advice is based on a model of how human meaning works that does not match how it actually works. The advice put you in the wrong job. You did the wrong job. The advice then makes you the villain of the result.

Mark's eight months are not Mark's failure. They are the failure of advice, paid in Mark's currency, in the only currency the advice has ever asked anyone to pay in: time you do not get back.

I want you to feel the size of that, because the size matters.

A great many of the men and women reading this book have spent some version of Mark's eight months — sometimes longer — circling. They circled as their kids got older. They circled while their parents were dying. They circled while their wife waited patiently to see what they would choose. They circled while the advice kept telling them they would know it when they felt it. They never felt it.

You are not weak. You are not insufficiently introspective. You are not failing at retirement, or at midlife, or at being a person. You are following advice that does not work. Putting the advice down is the move.

———————————————

I had my own version of Mark's for eight months. I am writing this chapter in part because of how nearly the advice took me down.

The advice came up constantly in the first year out of uniform. *You just need to find your passion.* It sounded reasonable. Harmless, even. It did not land right.

I remember sitting in a small office during one of those early career-transition conversations — the kind a recently retired officer is supposed to have, with people who are well-intentioned and who have helped a great many people in worse shape than I was. The man across the desk was kind. He asked me what I was passionate about. He probably had a script that began that way, and a notepad he was going to fill in with the answer.

I did not have an answer ready.

Not because I did not care about anything. Because the question felt disconnected from how I had spent the last two decades of my life. Passion was not how decisions got made in the world I had come from. *Mission* was. *Responsibility* was. *The team* was. The question the man was asking me came from a different operating system.

I tried to engage with it anyway, the way he meant it. I started making lists. Things I liked. Things I was interested in. Things I thought I should be interested in. The lists were diligent, as are most things I do. They were also useless. None of it stuck.

I remember looking at one of those lists, late one evening, and noticing something. The items were not connected to one another. The items were not building toward anything. The items were on the surface of an interior that, on examination, did not have a shape underneath them. I was not building anything. I was just circling.

That was the frustrating part. It felt like an activity. It was not progress.

I tried leaning into a few of the items anyway. Reading more. Exploring different paths. Nothing serious. Just enough to see if something would *click*. That was the verb the advice kept using. *Click.* Some piece of me would slot into some piece of the world, and a quiet sound would happen, and from there everything would unfold.

It did not click.

The thing I want to tell you, because it took me too long to figure out, is that the advice contained a hidden assumption I had not noticed. The hidden assumption was that there was a thing out there I was supposed to *discover*, and that once I found it, everything else would line up. The advice was a treasure-hunt model of the human soul. The treasure was real. The map was not provided. My job was to keep digging until I struck it.

The treasure-hunt model is wrong about how meaning is built. There was no buried thing. There was no hidden self. There were only the work I had not yet started, the people I had not yet decided to be responsible for, and the structures I had not yet built. The waiting was the problem. The waiting was the *whole* problem. While I waited for a click, I was not building anything. While I was not building anything, the absence of anything built was being slowly translated, in my head, into evidence that I was not the kind of person who builds things.

What eventually shifted things was not finding a passion.

It was stepping back into *responsibility.*

Work, in the form of joining Boeing, not because I was passionate about defense contracting, but because the work reconnected me to a mission, and the mission gave me people I was responsible for. Family, in the form of paying the kind of attention to my wife and kids that the squadron schedule had never quite let me pay. Building, in the form of starting a youth lacrosse league in my community, not because I was passionate about lacrosse, but because coaches had once mattered to me, and I could pass that forward. And, eventually, the Ph.D. — not because I was passionate about the field, but because I wanted a direction to grow into, and the program gave me one.

None of those came from asking *what am I passionate about?*

They came from asking *where can I be useful?*

That question is not in the advice. The advice has never been asked. It is the question this book is going to ask you, and the rest of the chapters are going to give you a way to answer it.

Let me say what is wrong with the advice, plainly, so we can name it and move on.

The advice mistakes the *output* of a meaningful life for its *input*.

Passion does exist. Passion is real. People who appear, late in life, to have lived a passionate existence — the great teacher, the lifelong scientist, the surgeon at sixty who still loves the work — are not lying. They are passionate about what they do. The advice notices this and gets the causation backward. The advice assumes the passion came first and the work followed it. *They figured out what they loved, and then they did it for forty years.* That is almost never how it happened. What happened, in almost every case, is that they walked into a piece of work for ordinary reasons — money, duty, accident, a parent, a teacher, a draft notice — and the work, over decades, made them who they are now. The passion is the result. The work is the cause.

The advice has it inside out.

You can confirm this in the people you actually know. Ask the men and women in your life who are most clearly *into their work* how they got there. The answers will not, on examination, sound like a treasure-hunt model. They will sound like *I needed a job, and my uncle worked at the firm.* Or *I was studying something else, and a professor handed me a problem.* Or *my mother got sick, and I started taking her to chemo, and I got interested in oncology.* Or *my best friend died young, and I started raising money for the foundation, and the work changed my life.* The doorway into the work was almost never a click. The doorway was almost always a small obligation, taken seriously, that got bigger.

Cal Newport, who has written more clearly about this than anyone in the last twenty years, makes the point as cleanly as it can be made: the people we admire are not passionate about their work because they found the work that matched their passion. They are passionate because they did the work long enough and well enough to get *good* at it, and getting good at something is the most reliable producer of meaning any human has ever discovered. [VERIFY: cite *So Good They Can't Ignore You*, Newport, 2012.] Angela Duckworth's work on grit makes a parallel point from a different angle: passion is not a found thing but a developed thing, and what looks from the outside like the person who *had* passion all along is, on examination, the person who showed up long enough for passion to appear. [VERIFY: cite Duckworth, *Grit*, 2016.]

This is not a small distinction. The treasure-hunt model leaves you stuck. The build model gives you something to do tomorrow.

Here is the build model, since this book will refer to it more than once:

You walk into a piece of work for ordinary reasons. You agree to be responsible for a small number of specific people inside the work. You stay long enough to get good at it. You let the work change you. Over the years, you notice that the work has come to mean something you did not, in the beginning, expect it to mean. The meaning is not the input. The meaning is the residue of the work, deposited on you by the work, over a long enough stretch of time.

Most readers of this book are forty-five, fifty-five, or sixty-two and have already lived long enough to confirm that the build model is how it actually goes. The work that has made you who you are was not work you were *passionate* about when you started it. It was work you took seriously. The seriousness, sustained, made the passion. You know this. You have just not been allowed to use it as a guide for what to do *next*, because the advice has been telling you, for thirty years of magazine covers and TED talks and graduation speeches, that the *next* thing is supposed to come from a different model entirely.

The next thing comes from the same model that brought you everything else worth having.

You walk into the next piece of work for ordinary reasons.

You agree to be responsible for a specific, small set of people.

You stay long enough to get good at it.

You let the work change you.

That is the chapter you are reading.

You may have three objections forming as you read. Let me answer them now.

The first: *but I do know what I love. The advice has worked for me before.* You are not the reader; this chapter is for you. If you know what you love and the love is sustaining you, do that thing. This chapter is not arguing with you. The chapter argues about a situation in which the reader has been told by everyone in their life to *find* something they cannot find, is now sitting in a garage with $11,400 in hobbies, and is being told that the failure is theirs.

The second: *but passion has worked for some people. I know a man who quit his job to become a sculptor and is now happy.* Yes. There are people for whom the find-your-passion model has produced a good outcome. There are also people who win the lottery. Both populations exist. Neither one is a basis for advice to people who have not won. The reader of this book is not going to win the passion lottery. The reader of this book is going to have to build, the way nearly every meaningful adult life is actually built, and the chapter is here to put the lottery model down so the reader can pick the build model up.

The third: *this is too cynical. There has to be more to life than usefulness.* I want to push back on the cynicism charge, because it is not what is happening in this chapter. The chapter is not anti-passion. The chapter is anti-*waiting* for passion to show up unbuilt. Building, when you do it long enough and seriously enough, produces the thing the find-your-passion advice promised. You will get to it.

You will not get to it the way the advice told you to. The cynicism charge belongs to the model that promised something it could not deliver, not to the model that asks you to actually do the work.

You are not going to be cynical at the end of this book. You are going to be *building*, which is the cure for cynicism, not its cause.

The practice for this chapter is one move, and the move is small, and the move will probably not look like much when you read it, and the move is, in my experience, the single most important practical change a stuck reader of a book like this can make.

You replace the question.

The old question was *what am I passionate about?*

The new question is *where can I be useful?*

That is the practice. The whole practice. Read it again if you need to.

Most readers, when they encounter this for the first time, think the new question is too modest. *Useful?* That sounds like settling. That sounds like a man who has given up on his dreams and is now resigning himself to volunteering at the church potluck. The reaction is understandable. It is also wrong. *Useful* is a deceptively large word. The work that has produced the great careers, the great families, the great communities, and the great inner lives of the last several thousand years has all been, if you look at it honestly, the patient sustained pursuit of usefulness to a specific group of people. The Ph.D. you respect was useful to her field for forty years. The grandmother who held three generations together was of great use to her family for six decades. The teacher you still remember was useful to one classroom of kids, year after year, for thirty-five years. The pastor was useful to a congregation. The squad leader was useful to twelve men. The founder was useful to a customer.

Useful, not passionate. Useful is the cause. Passionate is the effect. We have been confusing the two for so long that the word *useful* has come to sound smaller than it is.

So. The practice.

For the next week, when you catch yourself asking *what am I passionate about*, replace it. Out loud, in your head, on a notepad — the medium does not matter. The replacement is the practice.

Where can I be useful?

You will notice, immediately, that the new question is harder to dodge. The old question gave you permission to keep waiting until something showed up. The new question requires you to look around at the actual people in your actual life and the actual situations they are actually in. The new question can be answered today by anyone with eyes. It cannot be answered, ever, by anyone who is waiting.

You may also notice that the new question makes you slightly uncomfortable. That is correct. Discomfort is the cost of looking honestly at where you are needed. The old question was comfortable because nobody needed anything from a man waiting to feel a click. The new question costs you something. The cost is what makes it work.

If you want to see what the new question looks like when it is answered, look at the people you know who are not stuck.

The grandmother, who attends her granddaughter's piano recital every Tuesday at 4, is answering the new question. She did not find a passion for piano. She decided to be useful to a kid. The neighbor who runs the volunteer fire department on weekends is answering the new question. He did not find a passion for emergency response. He decided to be useful to a town. The retired doctor who consults for a free clinic two mornings a week is answering the new question. He did not find a passion for free clinics. He decided to help patients who would otherwise not see a doctor. The man at the church who has been quietly running the food pantry for fourteen years is answering the new question. He did not find a passion for food pantries. He decided to help families who needed groceries on Saturday mornings.

You will recognize, when you start looking, that the people in your life who appear most clearly *placed* are not placed because they found a calling. They were placed because they answered the new question plainly and showed up the next day and the day after that, and the placement became visible only in retrospect.

You can do that. The chapter is not asking you to be a saint. It is asking you to ask the new question.

The reflection for this chapter is short and concrete:

> *List five people, by name, who would notice if you went silent for a month. Friends. Family. Coworkers. Neighbors. The man who runs the deli. The woman who manages your team. The kid you used to coach. List five names, no more, no fewer. When you have them, star the first one you wrote down. That name is information. Save the list.*

You will be tempted to make the list aspirational — to write the people you wish would notice rather than the people who actually would. Don't. The exercise is diagnostic, not motivational. The five names are a partial answer to the new question; they are a sample of the actual web of usefulness you are already inside, whether you have been paying attention to it or not.

We will use the list in the next chapter.

A note before we close.

You have just done something that will look, in hindsight, like the most important move of the early part of this book. You have *put down* the advice that has kept a great many readers stuck for years. That is a small action. It is also a structurally large one. The room is now empty of the wrong instructions.

The next chapter fills the room.

If passion is not the engine — if the find-your-thing model is wrong — what *is* the engine? The next chapter is the answer, and the answer is going to sound contrarian until you live with it for a few days, after which it will start to sound, as the truest things tend to, faintly obvious.

The answer is *obligation.*

That is Chapter 4.

Chapter 4 — Obligation Is the Engine

The alarm was set for 0430.

I was already awake when it went off. That usually meant I had not slept well. I lay there a minute longer than I should have, knowing I needed to get moving, but not feeling any particular urgency.

The morning was routine. Pre-dawn training sortie. Nothing high-profile, nothing the squadron would mention by name in the day's debrief. Two F/A-18s, a marginal weather window, a young wingman, a brief at 0530, wheels up by 0700. The kind of morning every fighter pilot has flown a hundred times by the time he stops counting.

I went through the steps. Shower. Coffee. Flight suit.

The flight suit did something on most mornings. You zipped it up. You secured the cuffs. You slid the survival knife into the leg pocket the way you had slid it a thousand times before. A switch flipped. The man who had been a husband and a father at the kitchen table fifteen minutes ago was now an operator with a sortie to fly. The suit did the work of the switch. It always had.

That morning, the suit did not quite flip it.

I felt the absence. I noticed myself going through the motions instead of stepping into them. The boots were laced. The patches were squared. The body was prepared. The thing inside the body was not particularly cooperative. It felt, to use the most exact word I have for it, like *going through steps* rather than *stepping into something*.

The weather did not help. Low ceiling. Overcast. The kind of marginal pre-dawn that is not unsafe but is not clean — heavier than a normal morning, less forgiving, the kind of weather that makes a routine sortie quietly more technical. The kind of morning that asks for sharpness from the left seat, and on which I, that morning, was not yet sharp.

The drive in was quiet. I did not turn the radio on. I went through the schedule in my head — the timeline, the contingencies, the divert plan, the airspace deconfliction — and noticed that I was running the brief by myself in the car, not because I needed to, but because I was trying to wake up the part of me that flies the airplane. The schedule was not the problem. I knew the schedule. The problem was internal, and the schedule was not going to fix it.

I want to be careful, because the most honest thing I can tell you about that morning is that nothing happened.

There was no inciting incident. There was no breakthrough on the drive. There was no conversation with a buddy at the gate that snapped me into focus. There was just a man in a flight suit, in his car, at 0500, driving onto base, on a Tuesday in marginal weather, who was not particularly motivated to be doing what he was about to do.

And he did it anyway.

This is the chapter you are reading.

Here is the chapter's claim, said plainly so you can carry it with you for the rest of the book:

You do not move forward in the seasons of your life that matter most because of a lack of motivation.

You move because of obligation.

Inspiration is what every self-help book in the next aisle of the store has told you is the engine. It is not the engine. It is, in the lives of every adult I have known who actually moves through hard transitions, the *exhaust*. Inspiration appears, sometimes, after you have been doing the work long enough for the work to start producing it. Inspiration does not show up in advance. Inspiration is not a preflight check. Inspiration is what you discover, an hour into the sortie, that you have somehow developed.

Obligation, by contrast, is available before you feel anything.

Obligation is the wingman in the ready room who does not need you to be perfect but needs you to be steady. Obligation is the crew chief who has had hands on your jet since 0300. Obligation is your daughter at the breakfast table, who is going to ask you about her science project tonight. Obligation is the team you said you would lead. Obligation is the man you used to be at twenty-two, who does not deserve to be abandoned by the man you have become at fifty-four. Obligation is *people*. Specific people, in specific positions, with specific expectations of you.

You can run on obligation when motivation has gone offline. You cannot run on motivation when motivation has gone offline.

The contrarian claim of this book — and the engine room of the second half — is that obligation, properly understood, is not a burden. It is the most reliable producer of forward motion any human being has ever had access to.

That is the chapter you are reading.

The ready room was already moving when I walked in.

Coffee cups were out. Publications were open on the standby tables. Someone — the operations officer, probably — was flipping through the morning's weather brief at the front of the room, frowning the way pilots frown at low ceilings. The duty officer was on the phone with someone in maintenance. There were three or four other crews in there, prepping for sorties of their own. A couple of them looked sharp. A couple looked the way I felt. You can tell, in a ready room, in the first ten seconds, who is on and who is not. You don't have to be told. You feel it the way you feel barometric pressure.

I fell into the middle that morning. Not off. Not sharp. Middle.

There is a thing about ready rooms that I want to describe, because it does not get said outside of squadrons and it is exactly the thing this chapter is about.

You don't need to be motivated in a ready room.

The room is doing the motivating for you. The schedule is on the wall. The brief starts in 12 minutes. The pubs are open to the relevant chapters. Someone is checking the NOTAMs. Someone else is running a final weight-and-balance. The system is moving, and it has momentum you walk into rather than generate. You step into the system. The system carries you on most mornings.

The first face I saw was my wingman's.

He was younger than me by ten years. Solid pilot. Building experience. He was already at the table where we were going to brief, with his pubs open and his pen out and his eyes on the door, waiting for me. The thing he needed from me that morning — the thing his readiness was implicitly asking for — was not heroism. He did not need me to be the best stick in the squadron. He did not need me to be inspired. What he needed was for me to be *steady.* Just steady. Steady was enough.

I am writing this chapter twenty years later, and I can still see his face. The face is the part of the morning I remember most clearly.

I sat down. I opened my pubs. I ran the brief.

The brief took twenty-eight minutes. Timeline. Weather. Mission objectives. Roles and responsibilities. Contingencies. Communications plan. Divert fields. Bingo fuel. Emergency procedures. The brief was something I had given hundreds of times in some form, and, like all good briefs, it had a structure that did not require me to feel anything to deliver it. I delivered it. I asked questions. He asked questions. We talked through the technical stuff. We talked through the edges of the weather. We talked about the airspace.

Somewhere in the middle of the brief — I cannot tell you exactly when, because the shift was not dramatic — I noticed that I had stopped doing the brief and started *being* in the brief. The two are not the same thing. The first one is performance. The second one is presence. The second one cannot be willed. The second one can be walked into.

I think the moment I noticed the shift was when my wingman asked me about the contingency plan for losing communication during the egress. He asked it the way a younger pilot asks a senior pilot a question — looking at me, expecting an answer, not just to know the answer but because the answering of it was a part of how he learned to be in the air. I gave the answer. I heard my own voice. The voice was steady. The voice had not been steady in the car forty minutes earlier. Something had locked in between then and now, and the locking-in had not happened because I willed it. It had happened because I was sitting across from a man who needed me to be steady, and the *needing* had done the work the willing could not.

That is the chapter. That paragraph is the chapter.

By the time we stepped to the jets, whatever I had been carrying at 0430 was no longer relevant. Not because it had resolved. Not because I had figured out a meaningful way to feel different about my morning. Because the morning had stopped being about what I was feeling. The morning had become about what was being asked of me, and what was being asked of me was clear, and the clarity of the asking was, finally, more decisive than the murk of the feeling.

The flight was uneventful. I do not remember most of it. We flew the sortie. We hit the marks. We came home. He grew, I think, a little, on that flight, the way wingmen do when their lead lets them be challenged. I did not, at the time, recognize the morning as one I would still be writing about two decades later. It was just another sortie.

It is the most useful sortie I have ever flown, and not for any reason related to airpower.

There is a phrase about all this — half adage, half hard-earned wisdom — that I want to share with you, because it is a fair summary of what I am trying to give you in this chapter:

You don't rise to the level of your motivation. You fall back on the structure, the training, and the people around you.

That is the engine I am asking you to find.

The engine is not in your head. The engine is in the *room* — the room of obligations, of training, of people you have said you would show up for. When the morning is heavy and you cannot feel anything, you do not look inside for the missing fuel. You walk into the room. The room has the fuel. The room has always had the fuel. The work of the next several chapters is to teach you how to walk into your own room.

———————————

If the squadron version of the engine is dramatic — pre-dawn, marginal weather, an airplane — the civilian version is, almost always, quieter. I want to give you one.

Her name, in this book, is Carla. She is forty-six. She has not been in any uniform that anyone could see. Her last six months have not been chronicled in a press release.

Her mother is dying.

Not dramatically. Not with the kind of dying that prompts the family to gather around a hospital bed for the final scene. Slowly. Stage-four pancreatic, diagnosed eleven months ago, with a prognosis that is in the eight-to-twelve-month window, the doctors carefully avoid putting a number on out loud. Her mother lives in a one-bedroom apartment forty-three minutes from Carla's house. The apartment was supposed to be temporary — a place her mother moved into after Carla's father died three years ago, when she had not yet decided what came next, and which had quietly become the place she would die.

Carla is at the apartment three nights a week.

She does not enjoy these nights. I want to be very clear about that, because the find-your-passion model would tell her that if she really cared about her mother, she would *want* to be there. Carla does care about her mother. Carla does not want to be there. Both can be true, and one of them is the entire point of this chapter.

The drive takes forty-three minutes. Carla does not particularly want to make the drive on most of these nights. She has had a long day. She has her own kids. Her husband is patient about the schedule, but has begun to look tired in ways she does not have the bandwidth to address. The radio is on sometimes. The radio is not usually helping. She drives anyway. She arrives at the apartment. She lets herself in with the spare key her mother gave her in a moment of fragile lucidity in the second month after the diagnosis. She makes dinner. She handles the medication. She sits with her mother for two hours. She cleans up. She drives home.

She is not, on most of these nights, *inspired.* She is not feeling the *meaning* of these visits in the way the wellness culture would tell her she ought to be feeling it. She is, in the language she would use if she were honest with you, *tired.* Tired and uncertain and quietly grieving in advance of a loss she cannot yet absorb.

And she does it anyway, three nights a week.

She does it because no one else is going to.

That sentence is the chapter. *She does it because no one else is going to.* The obligation is not happening to Carla because she has located the part of her that finds dying-mother-care fulfilling. The obligation is happening to Carla because she has noticed, plainly and without illusion, that her mother is going to die alone if she does not show up, and she has decided that her mother is not going to die alone.

That is the engine. It is not a feeling. It is a decision about whose face you are unwilling to imagine missing.

What I want you to notice is how *available* Carla's engine is. She does not need to find anything. She does not need to discover a passion. She does not need a click. She has, sitting in front of her, an obligation that is unambiguous, immediate, and binding, and the binding is doing the work of the missing motivation.

You have a version of Carla's engine. So do I. So does Mark. So does Renee. The work of the rest of this book is to help you find yours.

Let me say what is happening, mechanically, when obligation works.

When you are obligated to a specific person — not an abstract one, not a hypothetical one, but a specific named person with a specific need — the question of motivation becomes irrelevant. You do not need to feel ready to call your sister back. You need to call her back. You do not need to feel inspired to attend your son's parent-teacher conference. You need to attend it. You do not need to feel a click before you make the trip to your dying mother's apartment. You need to make the trip.

Obligation outsources the question of motivation to a fact in the world.

This is what motivational systems lack. Motivation lives in your head. Motivation is subject to your weather. Motivation is sensitive to whether you slept well, whether the weather is marginal, whether the work felt small yesterday, whether your back hurts, whether the kids were difficult at breakfast, and whether your wife is angry about a comment from last Saturday. Motivation is unstable in ways that, by the time you are in your forties, you should have stopped pretending you can engineer.

Obligation is stable because it is *outside* you. Your wingman is in the ready room, whether or not you feel like leading him. Your mother is in the apartment, whether or not you feel like driving over. Your dissertation committee is meeting on Thursday, whether or not you feel like writing the chapter. The obligation does not move because your mood moves. That is the engineering miracle of obligation, and the reason it has been the engine of every meaningful adult life in the species' history.

The advice industry has spent the last twenty years trying to talk you out of using it.

The advice industry would prefer that you find your motivation inside, that you optimize your routines, that you stack your habits, that you align your incentives, and that you discover your passion. All of these are interior projects, organized around the assumption that what is missing in your life is *inside you*. That is, almost always, wrong. What is missing in your life is, almost always, *a clear set of obligations to specific people you have decided to be useful to.*

Restore that, and the motivation problem solves itself.

Lose that — and most people in their forties and fifties have lost that, often without noticing it happened — and no amount of internal tinkering is going to give you back what you lost.

I want to say something here that will sound, on first reading, slightly unfashionable.

Most of the unhappy adults I have known in my life are not unhappy because they have failed to actualize their inner gifts. They are unhappy because the structure of obligation in their lives has thinned out, often without their permission, often as a quiet consequence of accumulating success, and the thinning has left them in a place where no one is meaningfully counting on them for anything specific. The kids are grown. The team has been handed off. The parents are gone or being managed by paid help. The community is something they pay dues to and do not show up at. The spouse is a roommate they love but do not, in the daily logistical sense, *need*. The structure of being needed has been disassembled — sometimes by them, sometimes by life — and the disassembly has produced exactly the symptoms the wellness industry will tell them are caused by a lack of self-care.

It is worth noting, since most readers of this book are in the decade when this is happening to them, that the disassembly is structural rather than personal. The decade between forty-five and fifty-five is, for most adults in the developed world, the decade in which obligation naturally thins. The kids, who once required your physical presence at every meal, now require your texted reactions to their lives. The parents, who once relied on you for nothing because they were the parents, have begun — sometimes gradually, sometimes all at once — to need things from you that they had not previously needed. The work, which once required your hands on every part of it, now requires your judgment on a smaller number of high-stakes calls. The neighborhood is full of people you have known for fifteen years and whose names you know but whose phone numbers you have never had reason to use. The community organization you joined when the kids were small has long since stopped requiring your weekly attendance. None of this is anyone's fault. The structures of obligation that defined your thirties were built around the demands of your thirties, and your thirties are over.

The result is that in your fifties, on a Tuesday morning that should feel like freedom, you instead feel like nothing in particular is asking anything of you, and the absence of the asking is the loneliness you cannot quite name.

It is not a lack of self-care. It is a lack of obligation. The two have been confused for so long that we cannot, anymore, hear the difference.

Re-attach to obligation, and the self-care problem mostly resolves on its own. You sleep better when someone is counting on you to be sharp tomorrow. You eat better when you have a Saturday-morning workout with the men in your discipleship group. You drink less when your wife is the one who would notice. You move better when there is a place you have to be on Tuesday at six. The obligation is the cure. The interior optimization was always the wrong target.

That is the engine.

You may have three objections forming. Let me answer them now.

The first objection is: *obligation feels heavy. I am trying to escape obligation, not embrace it.* I hear you. The version of obligation you are trying to escape is, almost certainly, the version that has stopped feeling chosen. Obligation that has been imposed without your participation — by the workplace, by extended family expectations, by social structures you have not questioned — does feel heavy. I am not asking you to take more of it on. I am asking you to *re-choose* the obligations you already have. Choosing them, as adults can choose, makes them lighter. The same call to your aging father feels different when you have decided it is something you do, versus when you are subjected to it. The fact does not change. The relationship to the fact changes everything.

The second objection is: *isn't this just guilt repackaged?* No. Guilt is what you feel when you are not meeting an obligation you have not consciously chosen. Obligation, properly chosen, does not produce guilt. It produces *direction.* The clean form of obligation is when you have looked at the people in front of you, decided which ones you are responsible for, and shown up for them on the basis of that decision. The guilty form is when someone else has decided for you, and you are dragging the obligation behind you because you have not yet had the conversation with yourself about whether you accept it. The chapter is asking for the clean form. Guilt is the residue of the unclean form.

The third objection is: *I don't have anyone counting on me.* This is the rarest of the three objections, and the one that, when it is true, requires the most honest response. If you genuinely do not have a single specific person in your life who is counting on you, the work of the rest of this book is to *build* that. The chapters ahead, on the three channels of service, are exactly that work. But before you accept the third objection on its face, do the obligation audit at the end of this chapter and look at what you actually have. Most readers who think no one is counting on them turn out, on inspection, to have several people who are counting on them and to have stopped noticing.

———————————

The practice for this chapter is called the obligation audit, and it is, like most of the practices in this book, smaller than you will expect.

Take a piece of paper. Make a list. The list has one column. The column has one heading: *People who are counting on me.*

Then write names. Specific names. Not categories.

Not *my family.* Names. *Sarah, Daniel, Mom.*

Not *my team.* Names. *Mike, Priya, Jen.*

Not *my community.* Names. *Pastor Tom. The eight kids on my Tuesday-night U12 team.*

Most readers, when they do this honestly, find between eight and twenty names. Some find more. A few — and I want to address this carefully — find fewer than five. If you find fewer than five, that is information, and the information is the chapter you have just reached: the obligation structure of your life has thinned, possibly without your noticing it happened, and the rest of the book is going to help you re-thicken it. If you find eight to twenty, you have an engine. You have not been using it. The use is the work of the chapters ahead.

I want to acknowledge, before you start, that some readers cry the first time they make this list. Not because the list is sad. Because the names are a thing they had not, until that moment, let themselves admit they had been carrying. That is not a failure of the practice. That is the practice working.

For each name on the list, write one sentence about *what they specifically expect of you.* Not in an oppressive sense. In an operational sense. *Sarah expects me to be available by phone after 8 p.m. Daniel expects me to show up at his Saturday games. Mom expects me to call on*

Sundays. Mike expects me to be the steady voice in the team meeting on Mondays. Tom expects me to lead the men's group on Wednesdays at six.

The sentences will be more revealing than you expect. They will show you, in a quiet and concrete way, what your obligation engine is currently producing. The list will probably also show you, by what is missing, where the engine has been running idle.

Save the list. We will use it in three more chapters.

A note on what *not* to do with this list. Do not show it to your spouse. Do not turn it into a spreadsheet. Do not optimize it. Do not, in particular, try to *prune* it. The temptation, in a productivity-obsessed culture, is to look at the list and decide to "let go of" some items to "focus on what matters." Resist that. The chapter is asking you to see what is already there, not to begin re-engineering it. The re-engineering, if it is needed, is the work of the chapters ahead. Seeing is the work of this one.

The reflection for this chapter is one specific small action:

Pick one obligation from the audit list above. Honor it before noon today. (If it is past noon by the time you read this, before noon tomorrow.) Do not announce it. Do not make it bigger than it is. If the obligation is a phone call to your sister, make it. If the obligation is a conversation with the young engineer on your team, have the conversation. If the obligation is a visit to your mother, drive over. Notice what changed in your head between the moment before you honored it and the moment after.

You may notice, when you do this, that the smaller the action you take, the larger the internal effect tends to be. This is not random. The internal effect comes from the moving — from the fact that you, at one specific moment in your life, *acted on the basis of obligation* rather than *waited for the basis of motivation*. The acting is the engine. The first time you start the engine, the engine starts.

It is not impressive. It is not viral. It is not the kind of thing that turns into a TED talk. It is, however, the actual mechanism by which adult lives get back into motion when they have stalled, and it is the mechanism on which the rest of this book is built.

A note before we close.

Obligation gets you out of bed. That is most of the battle. But there is a second piece — a piece that reaches you ten minutes after you have gotten up, when the obligation has gotten you into the kitchen, and you are now, inevitably, going to ask the question *all right, but what am I supposed to actually do.* The answer the wellness industry will give you is *figure it out first, then act.*

The answer this book will give you is the opposite.

You act first. You figure it out as you go. The acting is the figuring.

That is Chapter 5.

Chapter 5 — Action Before Clarity

There is a specific kind of moment in the life of someone who is about to start something that I want to describe to you because most of the time, we get the description wrong.

The wrong description is the *vision* description — the one the magazine profile of the founder gives you. A lightning-bolt moment at 2 a.m., a sketch on a napkin, a clear-eyed view of what would be built, a confident set of next steps. That is not what most beginnings actually look like. That is what most beginnings look like in retrospect, after the thing has worked, told by someone who is now organizing the past into a tidy story.

The actual description is messier. The actual description is a forty-something man on a Saturday morning in the spring, sitting at his kitchen table in Nassau County, looking at a yellow legal pad on which he has written, in pencil, a list of approximate things, and noticing that he does not have a roster, a field, a coach, an insurance policy, a registration system, a budget, a sponsor, a uniform supplier, or a single specific kid signed up.

That is not the description of a man who is ready.

It is the description of a man who is about to start anyway.

Some years after I retired from the Marine Corps, I started a youth lacrosse league.

I'm new to starting a youth lacrosse league. I had never run a sports league in any capacity. I had no preexisting community of board parents, no prior nonprofit experience, no lawyer in the family, no preexisting roster of coaches I could call on. What I had was a vague memory of how much my own coaches had mattered to me when I was a kid — the discipline, the accountability, the way one or two good men had made it possible for the boy I was at twelve to become the man I would later become — and a quiet conviction that the kids in my new town needed what I had once needed, and that no one else, as far as I could tell, was going to build it for them.

That was it. That was the whole starting position.

I want to be precise about what I did *not* have when I made the first phone call.

I did not have a clear picture of what the league would look like in five years. I did not have a sense of how big it would get. I did not have a staffing plan. I did not have a fundraising strategy. I did not have, on the day of that first call, even a working name for the thing. I had a vague intention and a phone, and on that Saturday morning, the phone was the only thing I needed.

Most readers of this book are waiting for what I did not have before they start what they need to start.

They are waiting for the picture. They are waiting for the plan. They are waiting for the right moment, the right partners, the right pre-conditions to be in place. They will tell you, if you ask, that they are *being responsible.* That they don't want to start something half-baked. That they are going to "do it right when the time is right." Some of these readers have been in this posture for two years. Some have been in it for ten.

I am writing this chapter to tell you that the time is not going to be more right than it is right now, and that the way to get the picture you are waiting for is to *start* — because the picture is on the other side of the starting, and the starting is not on the other side of the picture.

That is the chapter you are reading.

Here is the chapter's claim, said plainly:

Action precedes clarity. Clarity does not precede action.

You have been told, by every well-meaning advisor in your life, the opposite. You have been told to *think it through.* You have been told to *make a plan.* You have been told to *be intentional.* You have been told to *figure out what you actually want before you commit to anything.* The advice is not insane. The advice is mostly correct in environments where the relevant information is already in front of you, and the work is to apply it. The advice is dangerous in the environment you are actually in, where the relevant information is not yet in front of you and *cannot be* until you start doing something that produces it.

In the environment you are actually in, the order is reversed.

You start something. The starting produces information. The information lets you adjust. The adjustment produces more information. The next adjustment is more refined. Over six months or two years, what you have been doing has begun to look like a thing with a shape, and the shape is closer to the right shape than any plan you could have written at the kitchen table on the first morning. Not because the shape was hidden in you and you discovered it. Because the shape was *built* by the doing, in conversation with the world, using information that did not exist until you generated it.

This is how every meaningful thing built by a forty-five-year-old in the last thousand years has been built.

Stop waiting for clarity. Clarity is not waiting for you anywhere. Clarity is a thing that is produced.

That is the engine of this chapter, and it is the daily practice of the rest of your life.

———————————

The first phone call I made for the league was to a man I half-knew through a mutual friend, who had once mentioned, in passing, that he had played lacrosse in college and that his son was now seven. I did not have his number on hand. I had to ask the mutual friend for it. The mutual friend asked why. I said I was thinking of starting a youth lacrosse league in the area. The mutual friend said *huh, ok,* and gave me the number.

I called the man. I introduced myself. I explained, in approximately forty seconds, what I was thinking of doing. I told him I did not yet have a plan. I told him I did not yet have a field. I told him I did not yet have a roster, a sponsor, an insurance policy, or any clue about how much it would cost. What I had, I told him, was a memory of what coaches had once done for me, and a sense that there were kids in the area who needed what I had once needed, and a phone, and his number on a piece of paper, and an hour on a Saturday morning when I had decided to make some calls.

He did not say yes immediately. He said *let me think about it.*

That was the first piece of information.

The information was not whether the league would work. The information was that this man, when given approximately forty seconds of pitch from a guy he barely knew, did not say no. He said *let me think about it.* That was a piece of information I could not have generated by sitting at the kitchen table planning. The information was generated by the call, and only by the call.

I made fifteen or so calls that morning.

Of those, a handful said something approximately like *let me think about it.* A couple said something approximately like *yes, what do you need.* One said *I think this is a great idea, but I don't have the time.* The rest were polite versions of *no.* By the end of the morning, I had identified a small group of men who were willing to help, in some capacity, with an idea for which I did not yet have a plan. The group, between them, had children, contacts, gym memberships, friendships, and one actual playing experience: coaching a younger team a few years prior. Out of those men, in the next several weeks, came the early bones of the league.

I want to be clear about what those first volunteers did, and did not, do.

They did not give me a plan. They did not solve the field-availability problem, the insurance problem, the registration-platform problem, the equipment problem, or the question of whether the local high schools would let our older kids practice on their fields when school was out. None of those problems was solved by the first phone calls. The first phone calls produced *people in motion.* The people in motion produced information about who else to call, what to look at, what would be hard, and what — to my surprise — was already mostly figured out by other communities and just needed to be borrowed.

Several months after that Saturday morning, we ran the first season.

It was, by any reasonable measure of organized sport, a barely functional season. We had about 60 kids across three age groups. The fields were borrowed from Parks and Recreation on a schedule that changed twice in the first month. The uniforms arrived later than I had been told they would. One coach quit two weeks in because his work schedule shifted. One parent became upset about a thing I cannot, at this distance, fully reconstruct, and stopped speaking to me for several weeks. The thing I remember most clearly about that season is that, at the end of the last Saturday — which was a sunny day in late Spring, on a field that was not quite the right field, with a small group of parents who had not yet decided whether they liked me — the kids did not want to leave the field. They wanted to know when the next season started.

That was the second piece of information.

The first piece was that the calls would generate possibilities. The second piece was that the work, even in its least polished form, would produce something worth coming back for. Both pieces were generated by *doing the thing.* Neither could have been generated by *planning the thing.* If I had waited until the plan was complete to start the league, I would still be waiting.

I am writing this chapter many years after that Saturday morning, and the league, in some form, is still going. Some of the boys who played in the early seasons are now coaching the program themselves. I am, by any reasonable accounting, the proudest of the messy first season I have ever been of a thing I did, because the messy first season is the only reason any of the rest of it exists.

I could not have written you the league description in advance. The description is the *result* of the doing. There is no version of the description that exists without the doing.

Most readers of this book are sitting on a version of the league.

A class they are thinking about teaching. A small business they are thinking about starting. A novel they are thinking about writing. A neighborhood circle, they are thinking about gathering. A nonprofit they are thinking about volunteering for. A church group they have been meaning to join for two years. A side practice they have been waiting to begin. The version varies. The structure of waiting is the same.

You are waiting for the plan. The plan is not waiting for you. The plan is on the other side of the first call, the first email, the first half-formed conversation with a friend on a Saturday morning. You are not lacking clarity. You are lacking the doing that produces clarity.

Make the call.

Let me give you the civilian version of this, because it is, in some ways, more useful than the league.

Priya is forty-nine. She has worked in operations roles at three different mid-sized companies over the last fifteen years, the last of which let her go in a restructuring she did not see coming, with a severance she had not budgeted for, and a quietly humiliating LinkedIn announcement she had to write at her own kitchen table.

She did the thing the laid-off-executive playbook tells you to do for the first three months. She updated the résumé. She had coffee. She met with the recruiter. She read the books. By month four, she had become aware of a pattern: every job description she found on LinkedIn was for either a job she had already done — and did not want to do again — or a job that was a half-step up from one she had already done, of the kind she did want, but for which her background was not, on paper, a clean fit.

A former boss of hers, a man she had not spoken to in two years, called her one Wednesday in May. He had heard, through someone, that she was open. He told her about a posting for a director-level role at a company in his network. The role was, on paper, half-aligned with what she had done. The other half was new. The salary was higher than she had been earning. The location was acceptable. The boss said, *I think you should apply.*

Priya looked at the posting. She did not, on examination, fully match it. She told the former boss this. He said, *Apply anyway.*

She applied.

She was not, in her own private reckoning, expecting to get the interview. The application was, she told her husband at dinner that night, *a thing I'm doing because Tom told me to.* She thought of it as a small action she did not believe in, taken because the man who had told her to take it had once been right about her career.

She got the interview.

In the interview — and this is the part of the story that, in my experience, almost no one expects — she discovered that the posting had been written for a role that, within the company, was slightly different from the one described. The written posting had been generic, drafted by someone in HR who had taken the previous occupant's job and copied half of it. The actual role, as the hiring manager described it across the table in the second hour of the interview, did, in fact, match Priya's experience cleanly. The half she had thought she did not match was the half they were trying to hire someone *into*, not someone *from.* They wanted to develop the person in the role; they did not need someone who had already done the new half elsewhere.

She left that interview with a job offer.

I am telling you Priya's story because the part of it that matters is not the offer. The part of it that matters is the *information* she could not have generated without applying. There was no version of Priya's home reasoning on the day she got the call from her former boss in which she would figure out — by sitting on her couch and analyzing the posting — that the role was actually a better fit than the posting suggested. The information was inside the room. The only way to get into the room was to apply. The application was the point.

She did not apply because she had figured something out. She applied because Tom told her to. The information arrived after she walked through a door she would not have walked through if she had been trying to plan her way to it.

That is the chapter.

Let me state the principle at the heart of all of this, plainly, so you can carry it for the rest of the chapter and the rest of your life.

Information is downstream of action.

The information you need in order to make a good decision about a piece of your life is, almost always, information that does not yet exist. It does not exist because it has not yet been generated. It will not be generated by sitting at a kitchen table, a desk, or a coffee shop and thinking harder. It will be generated only when you, at some specific moment in your week, take an action that interacts with the world and produces a response.

You do not need to plan your way out of stuckness. You need to *act* your way out of stuckness, and let the actions teach you what to do next.

I want to be careful not to overstate this, because the productivity industry has a version of *just take action* that is not what I am asking for. The productivity version is *hustle.* The productivity version is *bias toward action.* The productivity version is a kind of thrashing — moving for movement's sake, declaring that the moving itself is virtue. That is not what this chapter is about. This chapter is not about thrashing. This chapter is about taking *the smallest action that produces information.*

The smallest action is the practice. The information is the result. Adjust on the basis of the information. Take the next smallest action. Repeat.

That is the loop.

The loop is not impressive. The loop is not virtuous. The loop is, on most days, almost embarrassingly modest. The loop is a single phone call to a man you barely know. The loop is a single application to a job that might not be a fit. The loop is a single fifteen-minute conversation with the local school principal about whether you could volunteer to coach. The loop is a single email to the editor of the small literary magazine asking how to submit. The loop is a single afternoon of poking around in the basement, looking for the boxes of equipment from your father-in-law's retired contracting business. The loop is small, specific, and concrete.

The loop is also durable. Once you start running the loop, the loop accumulates. The phone call leads to another phone call. The interview leads to another interview. The conversation with the principal leads to a coffee with the athletic director. The email to the editor leads to a submission. The basement boxes lead to an idea. None of this is *planned* in the way the planning industry would have you plan. All of it is *generated* by running the loop.

The reason most adults in their forties and fifties have stopped generating new things in their lives is not that they have run out of capacity. It is that they have stopped running the loop. They have replaced the loop with planning. They sit at the kitchen table and analyze. They run scenarios. They list pros and cons. They wait for the moment when the decision becomes clear. The moment never arrives. The moment cannot arrive at the kitchen table. The moment can only arrive on the phone, in the room, in the conversation, in the application, in the small movements that the planning is not.

You do not need a plan. You need a loop. The plan, if needed, will appear on its own once the loop has run long enough to produce the information it requires.

Until then, the practice is just to keep the loop running.

It is worth saying what stops most people from running the loop, because the resistance is so reliable that it deserves to be named out loud.

The first thing that stops people is *the fear of looking foolish.* The smallest movable thing usually involves contacting someone, or asking for something, or showing up somewhere when you are not yet sure of yourself. The asking has a small humiliation built into it. The asking is an admission that you do not yet know. Most adults past forty have spent their working lives in roles where they are paid to know. The shift to roles in which they have to ask is felt in the body as a loss of status, even when no one else is watching. You will feel it. Take the action anyway. The looking-foolish is a small price for the information.

The second thing that stops people is *the fear of being told no.* If you ask, you might be turned down. The turn-down is felt as a personal verdict on the person, not as information about the situation. It is, almost always, the second of these. The first calls I made for the lacrosse league produced more polite no's than yeses. The no's were not verdicts on me. The no's were about who had bandwidth in that season of their lives and who did not. Treat the no's the way they should be treated — as data points to update on, not as judgments to absorb.

The third thing that stops people is *the absence of a clear definition of the action.* They do not start because they have not yet defined what counts as the smallest movable thing. They sit at the kitchen table waiting for the action to define itself. The action does not define itself. You define it. Pick the smallest concrete thing that produces a response from the world, and call that the action. Take it. Worry about whether it was the right action only after you have the data.

You may have three objections forming. Let me answer them now.

The first objection is: *I want to be intentional. I don't want to spend the next year just thrashing.* I am not asking you to thrash. I am asking you to take the smallest action that yields real information, and then use that information to adjust. That is not thrashing. That is the only kind of intentionality that is available to a person whose plan does not yet exist. The thrashing version of action is the productivity-industry version, and I am not advocating for it. The intentional version of action is *small, specific, information-producing, and adjusted on the basis of what comes back.* That is the practice.

The second objection is: *I don't want to waste years.* I hear you. The way to waste years is not to take small actions, gather information, and adjust. The way to waste years is to plan in your head for nine months at a time without ever interacting with the world that would tell you whether the plan is correct. Most readers of this book have already wasted some number of years that way. The chapter is asking you to stop. The wasted years are not behind you because you took action. The wasted years are behind you because you didn't.

The third objection is: *isn't planning responsible? Aren't I supposed to be careful?* You are supposed to be careful in the way that an airline pilot is careful before a flight. You are supposed to run a checklist. You are supposed to know the procedures. You are not supposed to refuse to take off because the perfect flight conditions are not present. There is a difference between *being careful* and *being immobile.* The chapter is asking you to be the first kind of careful. Most stuck readers, on examination, have been the second kind and have called it the first.

The practice for this chapter is called the smallest movable thing.

Pick a decision in your life that you have been paralyzed on for more than three weeks. Maybe it is whether to take the new job. Maybe it is whether to start the volunteer project. It's whether to apply to the master's program. Maybe it is whether to call the old friend you owe a call to. Maybe it is whether to talk to your wife about the thing you have been avoiding. Pick one.

Now identify the smallest concrete action that would produce *new information* about that decision.

Not a plan. Not an analysis. Not a journal entry. An action — small, specific, observable in the world, generative of a response.

If the decision is the new job, the smallest movable thing might be a fifteen-minute coffee with one person who has held the role you would be moving into. The coffee will yield information that no amount of staring at the offer letter will.

If the decision is the volunteer project, the smallest movable thing might be a single email to the organization explaining what you're willing to do. The email will provide information that no amount of research on the organization's website will.

If the decision is about the master's program, the smallest movable thing might be a 40-minute conversation with a current student. The student will give you information; the brochures will not.

If the decision is a friend, the smallest movable thing is the phone call. There is no information to be had from anywhere except the call.

Take the smallest movable thing.

The action does not have to take more than ninety minutes to execute. Most actions of this kind take less than thirty. The action does not have to be impressive. The action does not have to be brave.

The action has to be *specific* and *observable in the world*, and it has to *produce a response* that you can then use.

Take it today. Or, if today is past noon and the action requires office hours, take it tomorrow morning before 10 a.m.

You will notice that something changes after you take it. Not the decision — the *quality of your relationship to the decision*. The decision is no longer a frozen thing in your head. The decision is now a thing about which there is new data in the world. That is the entire move.

Repeat the move based on whatever decision is reached after the new data arrives. Keep repeating until the decision is no longer a decision, which is to say, until you have done it.

The reflection for this chapter is one specific small action, and the action is yours to identify:

> *Identify the smallest concrete action you have been avoiding be-*
> *cause you "haven't figured things out yet." It should take less*
> *than ninety minutes to execute. It should produce a response*
> *from someone or something outside your head. Do it before bed*
> *tonight. (If it requires office hours, before 10 a.m. tomorrow.)*
> *Notice what new information comes back.*

The point of the exercise is not that the action will solve the decision. The point of the exercise is that the action will *produce information*, and the information will move the decision out of your head and into the world, where it can begin to develop. That is the entire chapter, in one rep.

A note before we close.

You have just been given two of the chapter's three engines: obligation, in Chapter 4, which gets you out of bed; and action-before-clarity, in this chapter, which keeps you moving when you do not yet know what you are doing.

There is a third piece. It is the daily practice that holds these together. The daily practice is the title of the next chapter. It is a single phrase. The phrase is small enough to fit on an index card, which is, as it turns out, exactly where I am going to ask you to put it.

The phrase is *the next right step.*
That is Chapter 6.

Chapter 6 — The Next Right Step

Most of the practical wisdom that survives the years comes from a kind of writing that is not the kind of writing the bookstore tells you to expect.

The bookstore tells you to expect lightning bolts. Big revelations. The night the author's life changed. The book opens with a moment of crisis that ends in a sudden insight, and the chapters that follow are organized around the cleanup of the implications.

Most actual practical wisdom does not arrive that way.

It arrives at a desk.

Sometime in my early years at Boeing, on a Tuesday afternoon, I had an email open on my screen that I had been avoiding for nine days. I do not remember exactly what the email was about. I remember exactly what it represented. It represented a small administrative obligation that I had let slip through three or four reasonable excuses, into the territory of an obligation that I now had to deal with, not because dealing with it was hard, but because not dealing with it had begun to be its own form of work. Not dealing with it took up real estate in my head. Not dealing with it was a thing I was carrying around. Not dealing with it was a thing that, every time I opened my inbox, my eyes scanned past with a faint internal flinch.

It was a small email. Twenty-five-minute task, give or take. Nothing dramatic. No one was going to lose a job over it. No one was even going to notice, particularly, that I had been delaying.

I sat there for sixty seconds.

I want you to imagine those sixty seconds, because they are doing a thing that the rest of this chapter is built on.

In those sixty seconds, I was fighting nothing. I was not procrastinating by having a Netflix tab open. I was not stalling with a phone call. I was just sitting at my desk with the email open, in a state of small internal resistance, looking at a thing I had decided nine days earlier I would handle, and not handling it.

And then I noticed something I had not noticed before.

The sixty seconds were the obligation.

Not the email. The email was twenty-five minutes of work that, once I started, would be straightforward. The actual hard part — the part that had been costing me energy for nine days — was the *resistance to starting*. The starting cost is almost nothing. The not-starting had been costing me something every time I touched the inbox.

I clicked into the email. I handled the thing in twenty-three minutes. I closed it. I noticed that something had changed in my head between 1:42 p.m. and 2:05 p.m. that I had not been able to engineer through any other means.

That was, more or less, the day I started using the rule that became the title of this chapter.

The rule, as I have come to phrase it after twenty years of trying various formulations, is this:

Do one thing today that your future self won't have to fix.

That is the rule. That is the chapter. The rest of the next four thousand words are about why the rule is small enough to be useful and large enough to be the engine of the next ten years of your life.

Here is the chapter's claim, said plainly:

Forward motion in adult life is not a leap. It is a sequence of the right steps.

A right step is a particular kind of action. It has four properties.

First, it is *small.* It is not a big move. It is not a strategic pivot. It is not a six-month commitment. It is, at most, a ninety-minute thing. Most often, it is a fifteen-minute thing.

Second, it is *specific.* It is not "make progress on X." It is "send the email to Sarah about Y." It can be named in a single sentence.

Third, it is *defensible.* If someone watching your life from outside asked you, on a Tuesday evening, what you had done that day to move forward, the right step would survive the question. Not because it was impressive, but because it was real.

Fourth, it is *accountable to your future self.* The right step is something the version of you who exists in three months will be glad you did. Or, said differently, it is something the future you would not have to *fix* if you took it now. Most of what passes for forward motion in midlife is, on examination, the patching of things one's past self should have handled. The right step is the opposite: it is a thing the present self does, so the future self does not have to.

If you take one of these per day, for the rest of your life, you will not, in any conventional sense, be a person of inspiration. You will be a person in motion. You will arrive at places. You will build things. You will become, slowly and unromantically, the version of yourself you have been waiting to find.

That is the chapter you are reading.

I want to come back to the desk in Boeing for a minute, because I want to be precise about what the rule is and what it isn't.

The rule is not to *finish all your unfinished work.* That is, on most days, not possible. The rule is not *handle every email in your inbox.* That is, in some lives, also not possible. The rule is not *be ahead of your life.* The rule is, much more modestly: do *one thing.* One. A single concrete action. The kind that, once it is done, does not have to be done again.

The reason the rule is one thing, not three, is that one thing is achievable on a bad day.

Most rules of this kind fail because they assume the user is in a good state when applied. Most adults reading a self-help book are not in a good state. Most adults reading a self-help book are, on most days, running at about 65% of their nominal capacity, and the rules they are being asked to follow assume 100%. The user fails the rule. The user concludes that they have failed. The book is returned, and the user goes back to the same Tuesday afternoon, at the same desk, staring at the same nine-day-old email.

The next-right-step rule is engineered for the bad day.

On a bad day, you can do one thing. One thing is, in most lives, between fifteen minutes and ninety minutes of clear, concrete action. That is achievable for almost any adult who is not in a medical crisis. The rule does not ask you to be inspired. The rule does not ask you to be a better version of yourself. The rule asks you to identify one observable action you will not have to fix in the future. Almost any honest adult, on almost any day of their life, can produce one of those.

I started using the rule on bad days first. I used it on the days I came home from Boeing tired and could not face anything else, and yet had a list of small things accumulating that I had been letting go of, which were producing exactly the low-grade ambient guilt that the rule turns out to dissolve. *Do one thing.* Not three. Not five. Not a clean run at the list. One.

The first time I noticed the rule was working was about three weeks in.

I want to describe the noticing because it is what most readers of this chapter will be looking for and will not, on a daily basis, find.

The noticing was not dramatic. The noticing was on a Saturday morning when I woke up and, for the first time in some number of months, did not have an internal list of small, undone things quietly running beneath the morning. There were still some things to be done. There would always be unfinished things. But the undone things had stopped being a *background hum.* They had become, instead, a small, specific list that I would deal with the way I had been dealing with one thing per day for the last three weeks. The list felt different. The hum was gone.

That was the rule's first dividend.

I want to be honest about how unromantic this is, because the chapter will not work if I let you think the next-right-step practice is going to feel like anything for a long time.

It does not feel like anything for a long time.

For weeks at a stretch, the practice will be a series of small daily moves that you will not, on most days, notice yourself making. You will write tomorrow's next right step on an index card. You will take it. You will write the next one. You will take that one. The cards will accumulate. You will not, generally speaking, feel inspired about any of it. You will feel, instead, something quieter. You will feel like a person who is currently keeping the agreements they have made with themselves.

That feeling — the *keeping of small agreements with yourself* — is the actual emotional reward of the practice, and it is hugely underrated by the productivity industry.

The productivity industry wants to sell you bursts. Big mornings. Hyped-up Mondays. The four a.m. routine. The cold plunge. The supplement stack. The ritual that, if you do it correctly, will make you the kind of person who builds the company.

What actually makes a person who builds the company, or the league, or the marriage, or the body, or the book, is one thing per day, for ten years, almost none of it dramatic. The bursts are not the engine. The bursts are often what people do *instead* of the engine. The engine is small and quiet and, when it is running, almost imperceptible from the outside.

You are the only one who can run the engine.

You can run it tomorrow. You can run it this evening. In the next 40 minutes, you can take one specific, concrete action that the version of you in 3 months will be glad you took. The action is not on the productivity guru's list. The action is not viral. The action is, most often, a small phone call, a small email, a small conversation, a small repair, a small page written, a small file organized, a small bill paid before it becomes a problem.

That is the engine.

That has always been the engine.

The chapter is asking you to start using it.

I want to give you the most extreme version of this practice I have ever seen, because it teaches the modest version more clearly than anything else.

His name in this book is John. He is sixty-two. His wife of thirty-seven years died on a Friday in February.

I am not going to spend much time on the dying. The dying is its own subject and not the subject of this chapter. The relevant fact, for our purposes, is that on the Monday after the funeral — when the casseroles had stopped arriving and the relatives had flown home, and the kids had returned to their own cities and their own jobs — John found himself in the kitchen of the house they had shared for twenty-six years, alone, at 7:42 in the morning, staring at the coffee maker.

He did not know what to do.

He did not mean that in the existential sense. He meant that in the practical sense. He had no idea what to do that morning. There was no work to go to. There was no one to make breakfast for. There was no place he had to be. There was, in the immediate sense, nothing for the day to organize itself around.

His daughter, who knew him well, had handed him an index card before she flew back to Chicago. The card had three lines on it, written in her handwriting:

One walk.

One shower.

One phone call.

That was it. That was her instruction. That day, he was going to take one walk, one shower, and one phone call.

He took the walk first. He walked to the end of the block and back. The walk took twelve minutes. He did not notice anything in particular about the walk. He came back to the house and took the shower, which he had not particularly wanted to take, and which afterward he realized he had needed more than he had been willing to admit. He got dressed. He sat at the kitchen table and looked at the third item on the card.

He called his brother.

The phone call lasted eleven minutes. Most of the call was logistical. Some of it was not. He hung up. He noticed, sitting at the kitchen table, that the morning had become a thing he had moved through. Not a thing he had survived. Not a thing he had collapsed into. A thing he had moved through.

He took the card with him to bed that night. Before he went to sleep, he wrote the three items for the next morning on the back of it. *One walk. One shower. One phone call.* He did the three the next day. He wrote three more for the day after.

For ninety days, he did the index card.

I am writing about John not because his story is unusual, but because his story is the *cleanest* version of the next-right-step practice I have ever seen. He did not have anything else to organize his life around. The card was, in the most literal sense, the structure that kept his days together. Some of you reading this book have been through, or are going through, a version of John's morning. Most of you are not. But the principle that organized John's first ninety days is the same principle that organizes any next ten years of yours.

You write tomorrow's next right step on a card. You take it. You write the next one.

That is, on most days, the entire practice of being someone who is moving forward.

Let me say what is happening, mechanically, when the next-right-step practice works.

When you take one specific concrete action that produces a real result — and you do it today — three things happen at the same time, all of them invisible to the outside world.

The first is that you generate a small piece of *evidence*. Specifically, you generate evidence about *who you are.* You become, for a moment, a person who did the thing they said they would do. Most adults reading this book have, over the last decade, become people who did not do the things they said they would do. The accumulation of those moments has produced a quiet internal verdict that they are, on the whole, the kind of person who lets things slide. The verdict is not generally articulated out loud. The verdict is producing the stuckness. One small action against the verdict introduces the first counter-evidence in some time.

The second is that you reduce the *cognitive cost of being you.* Every undone thing in your life is taking up some amount of background processing power. The more undone things there are, the more background load. Most stuck adults are running a CPU at eighty percent capacity on background work that should not be background. One concrete action subtracted from that load produces a measurable amount of cognitive room. The room is what you have been wanting and have not been able to engineer with breathwork or apps.

The third is that you create *forward momentum.* This is the one most people understand, but most people misunderstand. Momentum is not a feeling. Momentum is a pattern of behavior. You do one thing today, and tomorrow's one thing is slightly easier to start. The day after, slightly easier still. The compounding is real, and the compounding is small, and the compounding is what produces the effect that, in three years, will look from the outside like a person who has somehow gotten their life together.

Compounding is also why most readers of this book do not have to overthink the *what* of the action.

Almost any next right step, taken honestly, will produce some version of the three effects above. The phone call you have been avoiding produces all three. The email you have not been sending produces all three. The walk you have not taken produces all three. The conversation with your wife, which you have been ducking, produces all three. The fifteen-minute file you have not been making produces all three. You do not have to find the *perfect* next right step. You have to find *a* next right step. The mechanism does not require optimization. The mechanism requires execution.

I want to push back, because someone is going to push back here, on the idea that small daily action is just *small daily action* and that nothing big can be built from it.

Most things big are built from it.

The book you respect was written one chapter at a time. The marriage you envy was kept together one Tuesday at a time. The body you admire was trained one workout at a time. The career that produced the dinner you went to last month was built one fifteen-minute task at a time. The lacrosse league I started with a handful of phone calls is now in its eighteenth season and was built one season at a time. None of this is small. All of this is composed of small. The smallness of the composition is not a deficit. The smallness of the composition is the whole engineering wonder of how durable adult lives get built.

Most readers of this book have been waiting for the leap. The leap is not coming. The leap is not how almost anything important gets done. The next right step is how almost everything important gets done.

You can take one tonight.

That is the engine.

You may have three objections forming. Let me answer them now.

The first objection is: *small steps feel insulting given what I am facing.* I have two responses. The first is that small does not mean trivial. A fifteen-minute call to a sister you have not spoken to in eight months is not a trivial action. The fifteen minutes do not measure the weight of the action. The second response is that the size of what you are facing is precisely why small is the right move. When the situation is large and unstable, the only operations that work are small, specific, and defensible. You do not steady a sailboat in a storm by making bold moves. You steady it by staying small and steady and accurate. Your life is the sailboat.

The second objection is: *I need to think bigger. The next right step practice sounds like I am giving up on thinking strategically about my life.* I hear you. The next right step practice is not the opposite of the strategy. The next-right-step practice is what makes strategy *possible.* You cannot think strategically about a life that is currently running a high background load of undone small things. The undone things will follow you into the strategic conversation and degrade it. Clean the background, by way of small daily actions, and the strategic thinking that you will then do will be sharper and more honest than any strategic thinking you have done in the last three years. The next right step is not anti-strategy. The next right step is pre-strategy. The strategy lives on the other side of the practice, not before it.

The third objection is: *this is just 'do something' advice in fancier clothes.* No. *Do something* is a posture. The next right step is a method. The method has four criteria — small, specific, defensible, and accountable to your future self — and a daily practice: write it down on a card the night before. The method is engineered. The advice you have been getting is gestural. There is a real difference between the two, and that difference is why the advice has not been working, while the method does.

The practice for this chapter is called the index card practice, and it is the simplest practice in this book.

You will need an index card. (Or a sticky note. Or a small piece of paper. The medium matters less than the constraint that whatever you use is small enough to hold one thing.)

Every night, before you go to sleep — not in the morning, not at lunch, the night before — you write tomorrow's next right step on the card.

There is a reason the writing happens at night. The morning version of you is not the right person to choose tomorrow's right step. The morning version of you is, on most days, processing input — kids, weather, sleep, the texture of the dream you just had, the news that arrived overnight, the eight messages that came in while you were asleep. The morning version of you is reactive. The morning version of you is also a worse honest broker about what tomorrow actually requires than the version of you who is closing out the current day. The night-before version of you has the day's data fresh in your head. The night-before version of you knows what is about to be on tomorrow morning's plate. The night-before version of you is making a decision for someone else — the morning person — and that gap is the engineering. The morning person, who would otherwise have resisted the action, now has it pre-decided, on the card, in last night's handwriting, as if it had come from a slightly wiser sibling. The morning person, who is bad at deciding, is good at *executing what was decided.*

The step has four properties. Small. Specific. Defensible. Accountable to your future self.

You put the card somewhere you will see it before you check your phone in the morning. The phone is doing a lot of work to keep you from running this practice; the card needs to win the morning before the phone does. Most people put the card on the bedside table, on top of the phone. Some put it on the bathroom mirror with a piece of tape. Some clip it to the coffee maker.

In the morning, you do the thing on the card. Do it before 10 a.m., if at all possible.

You do not do the thing because you feel like it. You do it because the card said you would, and you are practicing being the kind of person who keeps small promises to yourself.

That is the practice. That is the whole practice.

A few rules.

The card has *one item.* Not three. Not a list. One. The constraint is the engineering. If you put three things on the card, the card is no longer a next-right-step practice. It is a to-do list. To-do lists are fine. They are not what we are doing here.

I know it sounds insulting that the entire daily practice of an adult life is one card with one item. The insultingness is the test. The readers who can sit with the smallness are the readers for whom the framework eventually produces something. The readers who insist on writing seven items, or who upgrade the card to a Notion page, or who decide they need a different system to track the cards — those readers, in my observation, do not produce. The smallness is the practice. Honor it.

The item on the card is *something you can do.* Not something someone else has to do. Not something that requires a green light from someone you have not yet asked. *Send the email* is on the card. *Wait for Sarah to respond* is not. The card is your action, not anyone else's.

The item is *honest.* It is not what you wish you were, the kind of person who would do. It is what the actual you, on actual tomorrow, will actually do. Most people write the wrong thing on the card the first week, because they write the aspirational thing instead of the real thing. The card recalibrates over a few days. By the second week, you will be writing more honest cards.

The card is *for you alone.* You do not show it to your spouse. You do not post it on Instagram. You do not optimize it. The card is between you and the version of you who exists tomorrow morning, and no one else's input is needed.

A note about failure.

On some days, you will not do the thing on the card. The card will sit on the bedside table. You will see it. You will not do the action. You will go through the day with the card watching you. You will go to bed having failed your own small ceremony.

That happens. It happens to me. It will happen to you. Two rules.

First, do not throw out the card. Do not pretend the card was not there. Do not, in particular, decide that because you missed today, the practice "isn't for you." Most readers will be tempted to do exactly that. The temptation is the resistance to dismantling the practice on its own terms. Resist the temptation. The card is on your bedside table for tomorrow, regardless of what happened today.

Second, write tonight's card. Not as a "make-up" for the missed day. Not as an upgrade. Just write tonight's card the way you would have written it any other night. The practice is not perfect attendance. The practice is *return.* The thing that distinguishes adults who build durable lives from adults who do not is not that the durable ones never miss. It is that the durable ones return to the practice the next day without making a fuss about the missing.

Return is the practice. Perfection is not.

The reflection for this chapter is the practice itself, in its first rep:

Tonight, before you go to sleep, write tomorrow's next right step on an index card. One item. Small, specific, defensible, accountable to your future self. Place the card on top of your phone, or on the bathroom mirror, or wherever you will see it before you start the day. In the morning, do the thing on the card. Do it before 10 a.m. if you can. Notice what changes in your relationship to the rest of the day.

Repeat the practice every night for seven nights. By night three, you will start to notice that the writing of the card itself is doing some of the work. By night seven, the card will have started to feel like a small ceremony. By night thirty, you will not, on most evenings, remember a time when you did not write the card.

That is the engine of the practice. The engine compounds quietly. The engine is what the rest of the book is built on.

A note before we close.

You have just been given the daily mechanism that holds the rest of the book together. Obligation, from Chapter 4, is the engine. Action-before-clarity, from Chapter 5, is the principle. The next right step, from this chapter, is the *practice* — the specific daily move that turns the principle into a habit and the habit into a life.

You have everything you need to keep moving. The mechanism is now in your hands. The remaining chapters are about *where* to direct it.

The first three chapters of the book name the problem. Chapters 4, 5, and 6 gave you the engine, the principle, and the practice. The next four chapters give you the targets — the three channels of service in which an adult life rebuilds itself when the role that defined it is over.

The first channel is *work*.

That is Chapter 7.

Chapter 7 — Serve the Work

I want to tell you about the night I realized the cockpit was not the thing.

It was not, strictly speaking, a single night. The realizations of midlife rarely come in a single night. The realizations of midlife come in small installments, over months, until one of the installments lands and you notice, retroactively, that the realization has been building since the first one.

But there was a night — or a string of nights, blurred together at this distance — during the Boeing years when the realization landed.

I was at my desk at home. It was late. The kids were asleep. My wife was reading in the next room. I had been at Boeing for some number of months, and the work had been going fine, and I had been telling myself, with a determination that should have made me suspicious, that I was *grateful* for the work, that the work *mattered*, and that I was *adjusting* to the new uniform.

What I had not been letting myself say out loud was that I missed the cockpit.

Not the airplane. I want to be careful here. I missed the airplane on certain Sundays in certain weather, as any pilot does, but missing the airplane was not the thing. The thing I missed was harder to name. The thing I missed was a sensation that had been organizing my mornings for two decades, and the sensation was not, on examination, the sensation of flying.

The sensation was the sensation of being *useful to specific people.*

That is the sentence the chapter pivots on, so I want to give it room.

In the cockpit, on every flight I had ever taken, there had been a small, specific group of people on the other end of my work who depended on what I was doing. Sometimes the group was a wingman. Sometimes the group was a crew chief. Sometimes the group was, in a very direct sense, the Marine on the ground who needed close-air support to get home that night. The group was specific. The group was countable. The group was, in the most literal sense, *people I knew or could imagine knowing*, whose lives were going to be different, in measurable ways, because of how I did my job that day.

The cockpit had not been the thing. The cockpit had been the *delivery mechanism* for the thing. The thing was the specific people on the other end.

I did not have the language for this on Tuesday morning when I sat at the kitchen counter in Jacksonville. I did not have it for several months after. I had it on the night I am describing now — a night, late, at my home desk, when something quiet shifted.

The shift was this: I noticed, for the first time, that the work I had been doing at Boeing was not, in fact, missing the through-line I had been mourning. The through-line was still there. The through-line was the warfighter. The same warfighter who had been on the other end of every sortie I had ever flown was now on the other end of every contract review, every program decision, every conference room conversation, every Tuesday I spent on the systems that would, eventually, make their lives a little safer, a little better, a little more survivable.

The uniform had changed. The duty had not.

That was the night I started seeing the work differently.

That is the chapter you are reading.

Here is the chapter's claim, said plainly:

The first channel of service in the rebuilt life is *work*.

The work is not the same work. The work is, almost always, different. The work has a different uniform, a different cadence, a different room, a different paycheck. What stays is the duty underneath the work — the specific people on the other end of what you are doing, whose lives are different in measurable ways because of how you do your job today.

You will not, in the season after the role ends, walk back into the version of work that was the first version. That door is closed. That is not the door this chapter is asking you to walk through. The door this chapter is asking you to walk through is a different door, and the new door is harder to see at first because you have been told, by your culture and by your résumé and by your LinkedIn, that the door is the same one.

The door is not the same one.

The door is the *duty under the title* — the verbs you actually performed in the old role, stripped of the title that contained them, available for use in a new role.

The athlete who became a coach is using the same duty (transmitting discipline to people who need it) in a new role. The teacher who became a foundation director is using the same duty (making sure no kid is unseen) in a new room. The first responder who became an EMT instructor is using the same duty (showing up when other people can't) in a new room. The pilot who became a defense-industry program officer is using the same duty (being useful to the warfighter) in a new role.

That is what serving the work looks like in the season after the climb.

That is the chapter you are reading.

———————————————

I want to return to the Boeing years because I want to be precise about the texture of what *seeing the duty under the title* actually looked like in practice.

In the year or two after that night at my home desk, I started noticing the through-line in places I had not noticed it before.

There was a contract review I sat in on for a system upgrade — the kind of meeting that, before the night at my desk, I would have categorized internally as a "boring meeting about a thing I do at my new job." A few months after the night at my desk, I sat in the same kind of meeting and noticed that the upgrade in question was going to land in the hands of squadrons I knew, in airframes I had flown, on ramps I had walked across, and that the decisions being made in this conference room — by men in suits, in fluorescent light, with PowerPoint slides — were going to change the work-life of pilots I cared about, in ways the pilots themselves would never connect back to this room. The pilots would not know who had been at this meeting. The pilots would not know whose decision had improved the system. The pilots would eventually notice that the system was a little better, and they would fly with it without comment, because that is how the system is supposed to work.

I had, on every sortie I had ever flown, benefited from someone in that conference room who had, at some point, made a quiet decision that improved the airplane I was about to step into.

I had not sent that person a thank-you note on any of those sorties.

The realization landed in two parts. The first part was: *I have, for two decades, been the recipient of work in conference rooms I never saw, by people whose names I do not know, who were quietly being useful to me without my ever acknowledging them.* The second part was: *I am now in one of those conference rooms.*

Both parts changed my relationship to the work.

The work did not change. The decisions I was making did not, on any given Tuesday, look more glamorous because of the realization. What changed was my willingness to bring my full self into the work. The work was now part of the through-line rather than a parallel track. The through-line was the warfighter. The through-line had always been the warfighter. The through-line was just being delivered this season through a different mechanism.

I want to give you the practical consequence of this, because the practical consequence is the thing this chapter is actually trying to teach.

When I started seeing the work as continuous with my prior duty, I did it better.

Not dramatically better. Quietly better. I started reading the contract reviews more carefully because careful reading would benefit the warfighter later. I started speaking up in conference rooms I had previously been quiet in, because speaking up was a thing the warfighter would benefit from later. I started, in a way I had not previously done, treating the men and women in the conference rooms as colleagues in the same enterprise I had been in for twenty years, rather than as functionaries in a system I was now reluctantly part of. The reluctance went out of me. The work absorbed me. I noticed, sometime in the second year, that I had stopped grieving the cockpit. The grief had been replaced by something quieter and more durable, which was the recognition that I was still *on the duty.*

This is how serving the work works.

You do not find a new passion. You find the duty under the old role, and you ask, with honest eyes, where else in the world that duty is needed. The answer is generally not in the same building. The answer is generally in an adjacent building, doing similar work for the same enterprise. The athlete becomes the coach. The teacher becomes the principal, becomes the nonprofit founder. The pilot becomes the defense-industry decision-maker and becomes the policy advisor. The lawyer becomes in-house counsel and a board director. The shape of the moves looks like a career change. The shape of the duty does not change at all.

The reason most readers of this book are stuck on this chapter is that they have been mourning the *room* and missing the duty.

The room is gone. The duty is not.

This is also why retirement, in the conventional sense, almost never works for the readers of this book. Retirement asks you to step away from the duty entirely, on the assumption that the duty was an inconvenience that the work imposed on you. The duty was not an inconvenience. The duty was the thing that organized your life. You do not need to retire from it. You need to find the next room in which it can be done.

You have one. You may not have noticed it yet. But you have one.

A note about how long this takes.

Most readers want to know, on first read of a chapter like this one, how long the search for the next room actually takes. The honest answer is: longer than you want and shorter than you fear.

Longer than you want, because the next room is rarely the first place you look. Most readers spend three to nine months interviewing for jobs that turn out to be the old room with new wallpaper before they realize they have been looking in the wrong category. The old-room search is not wasted; it is part of how you learn what is and is not the next room. But it is not the next room. The next room reveals itself only after you have stopped looking exclusively in adjacent versions of where you just left.

Shorter than you fear, because once you start looking with the duty verbs in front of you instead of the old title, the next room often appears within six to twelve months. Not because the room was not there before — the room was always there. Because you were not, until now, asking the right question.

The right question is not *what is my next title?* The right question is *where else in the world are my duty verbs needed?* You will not find the answer by reading job descriptions. You will find it by talking to specific people who work adjacent to your old work and who can tell you where the duty verbs are in demand. The conversations are the search. The search produces the room.

<hr>

Let me give you the cleanest civilian version of this I have ever seen.

Her name in this book is Ramona. She is fifty-six. For twenty-seven years, she was a public-school teacher and then a school principal, in the same district, in two adjacent buildings, in a small city in the middle of the country.

In the last three years of her principalship, she burned out.

The burnout was not because she stopped caring about kids. The burnout was because the principalship — which she had loved for the first ten years, in the way one loves a hard job that gives back — had become, in the changes the district had absorbed, primarily an administrative role. She was managing budgets. She was managing her parents. She was managing the central office. She was managing compliance with three layers of state and federal mandates. She had lost, by gradual accretion, the part of the role that had brought her into education in the first place: the part where she walked the hallways at 8:15 in the morning and made eye contact with eight hundred kids and noticed which of them were having a hard week.

She noticed it, the burnout, on a Tuesday in May, when she looked at her calendar for the week and realized that she had no scheduled time, on any of the next five days, with a single child.

She handed in her resignation in June.

Most stories like this end here. Most stories like this end with the protagonist taking a year off, traveling, "figuring out what's next," and either coming back to a version of the same role at a different school or drifting into the kind of consulting that pays adequately and means nothing. Ramona did not do that. Ramona did the thing this chapter is asking you to do.

She asked, *what is the duty I have actually been doing for twenty-seven years?*

The answer, she eventually said in a conversation I am paraphrasing here, was *making sure no kid was unseen.* That had been the duty in the classroom in 1996. That had been the duty in the hallways in

2008. That had been the duty in the parent meetings in 2017. The duty had not changed. What had changed was the room in which the duty could be performed. The room — by the late 2010s, in the school system she was inside — was no longer compatible with the duty.

The room was the problem. The duty was still hers.

She joined a small literacy nonprofit eight months after she resigned, in a role that was, on paper, a step down — less salary, smaller organization, no executive parking spot. The role put her back into the hallways. The hallways had different kids in them. The kids needed the same thing the kids in 1996 had needed. Ramona is now sixty-two and is, in her own words, on the longest run of *being herself at work* she has had since her early thirties.

I tell you Ramona's story because I want you to see how literally the duty-under-the-title operation can work.

Ramona did not become a different person. Ramona did not find a new passion. Ramona did not retrain. Ramona did not, in any conventional sense, *pivot*. What Ramona did was strip the role of its title, identify the verbs that had mattered to her inside the title, and find a new room in which those verbs could be performed without the administrative apparatus that had made the old room unworkable.

That is the move.

You can do that move. The rest of the chapter will walk you through how.

———————————

Let me give you a different version of the same operation, because Ramona's situation is one in which the reader has financial latitude — she could take a step-down role at a literacy nonprofit because she had a teacher's pension and a paid-off house. Many readers of this book do not have that latitude. The framework still applies. The shape of the move is different.

Her name in this book is Mariela. She is forty-eight. She raised her son alone after his father left when he was three; the boy graduated from college eight months ago and lives, now, in another state. For twenty years Mariela worked as a hospital administrator in a midsize Southern city, the income paying for her son's tuition and her mother's late-life care and the mortgage on the small house where she still lives. She is not paying off her own retirement; her retirement, in any conventional sense, is not yet imaginable.

The hospital reorganized in the spring. Her role was eliminated. The severance was modest. She had three months of cushion and a son whose voice she missed and a quiet that, until then, she had been too busy to notice.

She did the verbs-not-titles exercise on a Saturday morning at her kitchen table.

The title at the top of the page was *hospital administrator.* The verbs underneath, when she was honest, were not the role's official tasks. They were the things she had been doing inside the role that mattered to her. *Walked the floor on Tuesdays. Knew the night-shift nurses by name. Translated for the Spanish-speaking families on intake. Caught the small operational failures before they became patient-care failures. Stood with the new hires through their first hard week.*

The duty under the title was *making sure no one in the building was unseen.*

She is not, today, the hospital administrator. She is, six months later, a part-time patient liaison at a community health clinic that pays her two-thirds of what the hospital paid. The clinic is on a bus line. The work is the work the duty verbs port to. The reduced income is real and is its own kind of difficulty. The duty has not changed.

Mariela is not the version of the duty-under-the-title move that the conventional second-act book describes, because the conventional book imagines a reader with margin. Mariela had no margin. The framework still worked, in the smaller and more constrained version of itself she could afford.

Most readers of this book are not going to take a literacy-nonprofit pay cut. Some of you cannot afford to. The duty verbs port anyway, into whatever room the reader can actually walk into. The work of the framework is to find the room you can afford, not the room the conventional book imagines.

––––––––––––––––––––

Let me say what is happening, mechanically, when serving the work works.

Most readers, when they start looking for their next channel, make the same mistake. They look at their old job title, and they ask, *what is the next title?* They look at their old industry, and they ask, *what is the adjacent industry?* They look at their résumé, and they ask, *what is the natural next line on the résumé?*

These are the wrong questions.

They are the wrong questions because they assume that the *thing that made the old role meaningful* is the title, the industry, and the résumé. The thing that made the old role meaningful is none of those. The thing that made the old role meaningful is the *verbs you performed inside it that delivered something real to specific people on the other end.*

The verbs are portable. The titles are not.

A school principal performs a few hundred verbs in a typical week. Among them: *budget. Manage. Convene. Hire. Fire. Discipline. Comply. Report. Walk the halls. Notice the kid in the corner. Listen to the angry parent. Listen to the teacher who is exhausted. Make the call about the substitute. Decide which fight is worth having with the central office. Stand in the lobby on the first day of school.* Of these, some are *role* verbs — verbs the title required because the title was the title. Others are *duty* verbs — verbs the person performed because the person was, underneath the title, the kind of person who did them.

The duty verbs are portable. The role verbs are not.

You will, in the next several weeks, be tempted to think you cannot find a next channel because the role verbs will not, on examination, port to anywhere else. You are right about the role verbs. You are wrong about the duty verbs. The duty verbs port. They have always ported. They are how every meaningful second act in the history of work has been built.

I want to give you a practical heuristic for finding your duty verbs.

Make a list of the verbs you performed in your old role. Be honest. Make the list long.

Now, for each verb, ask: *if I had performed this verb to a higher standard than was required by the role, who specifically would have benefited?*

If the answer to that question is *no one in particular* or *the company* or *my boss*, the verb is a role verb. It can stay in the old role. You do not need to bring it forward.

If the answer is *a specific person on the other end of the verb who would have noticed,* the verb is a duty verb. The duty verb is what you bring forward.

When you do this exercise honestly, the list of duty verbs will be shorter than the list of role verbs. That is correct. Most of what you did at the old job was role work. The duty work was a smaller core. The smaller core is the through-line. The smaller core is what you take into the next channel.

The next channel is almost always where the duty verbs are needed by the same kinds of specific people who used to need them in the old role.

The next channel is, almost always, *closer to the work than the old room was.* The old room had administrative scaffolding around the work that was, in the late stages of the role, taking up most of your time. The next room often has less scaffolding. The next room often pays less. The next room often has a smaller budget. The next room often, paradoxically, lets you do the duty work you went into the field to do twenty years before.

Most readers of this book, if they are honest, will find that the next room is *closer to the original reason they entered the field* than the room they have just left.

That is not a coincidence. That is the structure of an honest second act.

You return to your duty.

The duty is the chapter you are reading.

You may have three objections forming. Let me answer them now.

The first objection is: *I don't know what's portable about my old role. The role was the role. There is nothing underneath.* I hear you. The "nothing underneath" feeling is, almost always, an artifact of having stopped looking. You spent twenty years inside a role. The role required of you is a few hundred specific verbs, performed thousands of times each. The verbs that recurred most often were not random; they were the ones the role kept asking you for, week after week, year after year. Those verbs are the duty. They are not invisible. They are visible if you sit down with a yellow pad and make the list. The first time you make the list, you will think it is short. The list is not short. The list is just unfamiliar to look at, because you have been performing the verbs without naming them for two decades.

The second objection is: *what if my old role was just the role? What if there is genuinely no duty underneath?* Some readers will worry about this. Almost none of the readers who worry about it are correct. The way to know is to do the exercise — the verb list — and look at it honestly. If there are no duty verbs on the list, you are in a small minority of readers, and the rest of the book is going to be useful to you for different reasons. But before you accept that you are in that minority, do the exercise. Most readers who fear they have no duty verbs find, on inspection, that they have several and have been minimizing them.

The third objection is: *the next room sounds like it pays less, requires less status, and is harder to explain at parties.* Yes. All three are often true. The next room is, on average, of lower status than the old room. The next room is, on average, less recognizable on a résumé. The next room is, on average, harder to explain to a brother-in-law at Thanksgiving. None of those facts is in the chapter you are reading. The chapter you are reading is about the *duty.* The duty does not care about status, résumé, or Thanksgiving conversations. The duty cares about the specific people on the other end of your work. If those people are getting more of you in the new room than in the old, the new room is the right room. The status issue is real, and the chapter is not pretending otherwise. The status issue is not, however, the determining factor. The duty is.

The practice for this chapter is called *verbs not titles.*

It is the most useful single page of work you will do in the entire book.

Take a piece of paper. (The same kind you have been using for the other practices. Plain. Unlined or lined, your call.)

At the top of the page, write the title of the most recent role you wore — the one whose ending is what brought you to this book. *Chief Marketing Officer. Senior Vice President of Operations. Lieutenant Colonel, USMC. Pastor. Kindergarten Teacher. Principal of Springfield Middle School. Founder and CEO of Acme Corp.* Whatever your version is. Write it big at the top.

Now, in the body of the page, list the verbs you actually performed inside that role.

Be specific. Not *led the team — ran a thirty-minute Monday standup, took the senior people to lunch quarterly, sent the personal birthday email to each of the forty-three people on my team, walked the floor on Friday afternoons.* The smaller the unit of verb, the more useful the list.

Aim for thirty verbs. Some will be small. Some will be large. Most will be repeated several times a week without you noticing them. Make the list long enough that, on the page, the role is broken down into its actual operations rather than its titular shape.

Now, for each verb, ask the question: *if I had performed this verb to a higher standard than the role required, who specifically would have benefited?*

Mark the verbs whose answer is a *specific named person or kind of person* on the other end. Cross out the verbs whose answer is the company, the role, the abstract organization, or no one in particular.

The verbs you have marked are your *duty verbs.*

Of the marked verbs, circle the three that, on honest reflection, you would *most miss* if you never performed them again.

Those three verbs are the through-line of your work life.

They are the things to look for in the next channel. They are the things to keep doing in any new room, regardless of what the title of the room is. They are, more than anything else, the *reason you went into the field in the first place,* hidden inside the role you have just stopped wearing.

Save the page. We will use it again in two more chapters.

The reflection for this chapter is the *verbs not titles* practice in its most condensed form:

> *On a single page, write the title of your most recent role at the top. Below it, list the verbs you actually performed in that role. From those verbs, circle the three that, on honest reflection, you would most miss if you never performed them again. Those three are your duty verbs. Save the page.*

Most readers, when they do this honestly, find that the three verbs are *not* the verbs the title would suggest. The CMO's three duty verbs are not, on inspection, *managed brand strategy, oversaw advertising spend, and ran the marketing department.* The CMO's three duty verbs are something more like *helped young people on my team build careers, told the truth in board meetings about what was working and what wasn't, and made the work more honest than it would have been without me.* The duty verbs almost always describe a *quality* of work the title performed, not the title's *category.*

The duty verbs are the through-line. The duty verbs port to a thousand new rooms. The job of the next several months of your life is to find the room.

Save the page.

A note before we go on.

You have just done the first of the three channels. *Serve the work.* You found the duty under the old title. You named it. You wrote it down. The duty is now portable in a way it was not, on the morning the role ended.

There is a temptation, after doing this, to over-rely on the work channel. The temptation is real, and it is dangerous. A reader who solves the work channel and then runs only on it will, within eighteen months, have rebuilt some version of the original problem — because work alone, even meaningful work, was never the full picture. There were always two more channels under the structure of the old life that the role was filling without you noticing.

The next channel is *community.* Local. Specific. Built. The kind of channel that, without it, the work channel will quietly hollow out a second time.

That is Chapter 8.

Chapter 8 — Serve the Community

I want to tell you about a Saturday night in early summer.

I had driven home from a lacrosse field. The field was not particularly nice. It was a field the parks department had let us use, with lines that needed repainting, one corner with a permanent low spot that filled with water after rain, and a fence on the third-base side of the adjacent baseball diamond that we had to work around. We had run two games on it that day, an under-twelve and an under-fourteen, and the games had been the way Saturday games are: parents in folding chairs, coaches in baseball caps, kids in mismatched practice gear because the uniforms were still being washed from last weekend, three or four refs who had been driving from field to field since 8 a.m. and were running on a kind of caffeinated optimism that holds up only because the kids are still fresh.

The games were unremarkable.

I want you to hold that word, *unremarkable.* It is doing the work of the chapter.

The under-twelve game had a kid score his first goal of the season — a wobbly little shot from about ten yards out that beat a goalie who had been distracted by something on the sideline — and the kid had run to his dad's chair afterward as though he had won the World Cup. The under-fourteen game had been close enough to be tense in the third quarter and had been won by the team that wanted it slightly more. A coach had cried on the sideline because his son, whom he had been coaching for four seasons, had played the best game of his life. A girl I will call Hannah, who had been struggling with confidence all season, made one really good defensive play that did not show up on the stat sheet, but her mother, who I happened to be standing next to, noticed.

These are not the moments that get written about.

These are the moments that *make* a community, and almost no one writes about them because the people having them are too busy folding chairs, packing snacks, getting kids to dentist appointments, and buying groceries on the way home.

I drove home. The light was the kind of light you get in early summer, an hour before sunset, that makes everything ordinary look slightly more honest. I was tired. I had been in the field since 9 a.m. I had not, in any conventional sense, *accomplished* anything that day that would show up on a résumé.

And somewhere, on the drive, I noticed that I was answering a question I had not been able to answer at my desk.

The question was *what am I doing here.*

I had been carrying that question, in some form, since the day the uniform came off. I had been carrying it in Boeing conference rooms. I had been carrying it on early mornings in Jacksonville. I had been carrying it through the first eighteen months of the league, as the league grew and faltered and grew again. I had not been able to answer it from a desk. I could not fully answer it on this drive home. But the question was *quieter* than it had been.

The quietness was the league's first dividend.

That is the chapter you are reading.

Here is the chapter's claim, said plainly:

The second channel of service in the rebuilt life is *community.*

Community is not the word the wellness industry uses. The wellness industry uses words like *connection*, *belonging*, and *tribe*. Those words point at the same thing the community points at, but they point at it as a feeling. Community is not a feeling. Community is a *practice*. Community is something you build, in a specific local place, for a specific group of people, over a long enough period of time that the building becomes part of who you are.

You do not find community. You build it.

You build it by showing up, on a regular cadence, at a place you have decided to be useful to a specific group of people who would notice if you were not there. The cadence is the practice. The specific group is the membership. The place is the place. You do not need a vision statement for this. You do not need a website. You do not need a 501(c)(3). You need to show up. Then to show up again. Then again, the next week, even when you do not feel like it.

What the community delivers when you build it is not connection. Connection is the byproduct. What community delivers is *roots*. The kind of roots that, when the work channel falters or the family channel changes shape, keep you in place. The roots are the structural piece of the rebuilt life that the work channel cannot supply, even at its best.

That is what serving the community looks like.

That is the chapter you are reading.

Let me come back to the league.

I want to be precise about what the league does for me — not because the league is unusual, but because the structure of what it does mirrors that of every community-channel project this chapter asks you to consider building.

The league is, by any external measure, a very ordinary thing. It is a youth sports program in a moderately sized town, run mostly by volunteers, on borrowed fields, with a budget so small it would be embarrassing if I were ever asked to publish it. There are several thousand similar programs in the country. The league is not, in itself, special.

What the league delivers — to the kids, to the parents, to the coaches, and to me — is structurally important.

For the kids, it delivers what coaches deliver everywhere: the experience of being seen by a non-parent adult on a regular schedule, getting feedback on a thing that matters, being held to a standard, and learning how to be on a team. These are the things my coaches gave me when I was the kid running around on someone else's borrowed field, and these are the things I wanted to pass forward. The pass-forward is the pass-forward. It works the way it has worked for the four or five thousand years humans have been running organized youth activities, and it works because the structure is good, not because anyone running it is special.

For the parents, the league offers something almost no one writes about: *a place to be* on Saturday mornings. Saturday morning, in a community that has thinned out the way most American communities have, is one of the loneliest mornings of the week for a great many parents. The league gives them somewhere to go. It gives them other parents to stand next to. It gives them a structure within which their kid is being competently looked after by someone other than them. That is no small thing. The parents at the field on Saturday morning are, by their presence, building a piece of their own community channel without naming it that way.

For the coaches — most of whom are the dads of kids who are or were on the teams, and a few of whom are men whose kids have aged out and who keep coming back — the league delivers a *use for them.* Most of the men who coach in the league are, by midweek, running on something like Renee's CMO mug. They have careers that are fine. They have marriages that are fine. They have the same low-grade stuckness most readers of this book have. On Saturday mornings, with a clipboard in one hand and a whistle around their

neck, they are something specific to a specific group of kids, in a way
the rest of their week does not always let them be. The clipboard
is a uniform. The clipboard is doing what the lanyard at the office
stopped doing.

For me, the league delivers what I am actually trying to teach you
in this chapter: the *roots*. I am writing this chapter many years after
the first season. I have moved through several professional roles in
the last twenty years. The professional rooms have changed. The
league has not. The Saturday mornings have continued. Some of the
kids I coached in the first season are now bringing their own kids to
the program. Some of the original coaches are now grandparents
standing on the sideline. The thing I built in Nassau County, after I
made a few phone calls on a Saturday morning many years ago, is
now a fixed point in the town's local geography, and that fixedness is
doing something for me that no professional achievement has ever
done.

It is keeping me planted.

I want to tell you about one specific Saturday, because the specific
is more useful than the abstract.

Several years into the league, I showed up to a game I was not
coaching. My own kids had aged through the program by then. I
had been doing administrative work for the league in the off-season
— registration, scheduling, parent emails — but had not been on the
sideline of an actual game in some weeks. I was just there as a spec-
tator that morning, on a borrowed field, in a folding chair, drinking
coffee from the same kind of paper cup I had been drinking from for
years.

One of the boys on the field was a kid I had coached in his first
season, when he was eight. He was now thirteen. He had grown
about a foot. He had become, in the time I had not been watching
him week to week, a competent young player. He saw me on the
sideline. He raised his stick in a small wave, the way teenage boys
wave when they are too cool to wave but want you to see them. I

waved back.

That was the whole moment.

I am writing this chapter many years later, and I can still see his face. I cannot tell you why that wave is the one that stuck. It is what stuck. It stuck because, in that very small moment, the league had become something larger than the thing I had been organizing. It had become a place where a boy I had once coached, and who I had not seen for several seasons, and who was now nearly grown, knew me. And I knew him. And the knowing had been built, not through any single dramatic intervention, but through dozens of unremarkable Saturday mornings, on borrowed fields, with coffee in paper cups.

That is what community delivers.

That is what no professional channel, by itself, ever can.

Tom's version of community is quieter than mine, and probably more typical of what most readers of this book will end up building.

He is fifty-eight. He retired from the fire department after thirty-one years. He was a captain at the end. He took the pension on a Friday in March, walked out of the firehouse with a small paper sack of personal effects and a handshake from the chief, and went home.

For the first year, he did not volunteer for anything.

I want to spend a moment on that year, because that year is most readers' year, and almost no self-help book talks about it honestly.

He drank a little more than he wanted to. He watched too much news. He looked at his garage for several months, considered a project, did not start it. He had coffee with friends from the fire department, the way retired firefighters do, but the coffees thinned out in month four, because the firefighters were still working and Tom was no longer sharing the same Tuesdays they were. He tried a fitness routine that lasted six weeks. He read three books on retirement and recognized himself in about 1.5 of them. He told his wife he was *figuring it out.* He was not figuring it out.

His wife, gently, in month nine, told him over dinner that he seemed less like himself than she had ever seen him. He did not argue with her. He went to bed that night and, for the first time in some months, was unable to sleep.

The next morning he drove past the public library on the way to the grocery store and noticed a sign that read *American Heart Association Hands-Only CPR Demonstration This Saturday 10 a.m. Free Admission.* The sign was not aimed at him. The sign was aimed at the kind of community member who might come learn CPR for fifteen minutes on a Saturday morning so they could feel briefly virtuous. Tom kept driving.

But the sign sat with him for the rest of the day.

The next morning, he called the library. He did not know why he was calling. He told the woman who answered that he had thirty-one years as a paramedic and firefighter, that he was retired now, and that he had seen the sign about the CPR demonstration. He asked, in the awkward way of a man asking for permission to be useful, whether the library would have any interest in a longer-format class. He could teach it. Free, he added, before she could ask. Once a month, if she wanted. He had time.

She said yes.

The first class had four people in it. Three of them were elderly women who had read the flyer at the library. One was a teenage boy whose mother had heard about Tom through a neighbor. The class went for ninety minutes. Tom taught what he had been teaching to firefighters for fifteen years. He left the library that morning with the strangest sensation, which was that the sensation he had been missing for ten months had been *being needed by people he could see.*

The class is now a permanent fixture at the library. It runs on the second Sunday of every month. It typically has between 8 and 25 people in it. Tom is sixty-three now. He has not, in his own words, been this happy in a decade.

That is what community delivers.

It does not deliver flash. It does not deliver scale. It does not deliver a story that gets retold on LinkedIn. It delivers, on a Sunday morning, a roomful of specific people who needed something Tom could give them, and the giving of it.

Most readers of this book have a version of Tom's class waiting for them.

The work of the chapter is to find it.

———————————

Tom's version of the community channel works because he had the body for it. Some readers of this book will not. I want to give you a composite who has more limitations and for whom the framework still works, in a different shape.

His name in this book is Frank. He is sixty-three. He worked in fabrication and welding for forty-one years. He retired at sixty-two, not because he wanted to but because his back, which had been telling him for a decade that the work was using him up, finally became something the orthopedist could not fix. He cannot, on most days, stand for more than twenty minutes. He cannot lift anything heavier than a gallon of milk.

His retirement income is Social Security plus a small union pension. He lives in a house he and his wife paid off in 2009. They have grown children but no grandchildren yet. He has many of the same retirement-shape problems as the men in this book who retired from corporate roles, but with substantially less margin and substantially less mobility.

The community channel, in the form most self-help books describe — coach the team, lead the men's group, build the youth program — was largely off the table for Frank. His back would not let him. The forms of community service he had assumed he would do when he stopped working were no longer available to him.

What he found, after a year of feeling useless about it, was a community college that ran an introductory metalworking course for adult continuing-education students. He was not strong enough to do the work. He was, however, strong enough to *teach* the work, sitting on a stool, walking students through their first cuts and welds at a slow pace that his back could survive. The college pays him hourly — modestly, but it pays. He teaches one section a semester. He is, by his own account, the most himself he has been since he stopped working.

I tell you Frank's story because the community channel does not require an able body, a financial cushion, or a leisurely retirement. The community channel requires that you find a place where your duty verbs are needed in a form your current life can actually deliver. For Frank, that meant teaching from a stool. For another reader it might mean phone calls instead of in-person, weekend mornings instead of weeknight evenings, or one-on-one mentoring instead of leading a group.

The constraint is the constraint. The duty finds the form.

Let me say what is happening, mechanically, when serving the community works.

The community channel does something the work channel cannot, and the work channel does something the community channel cannot; both are needed.

The work channel produces *output* — products, services, decisions, results. Output is real. Output is necessary. Output is what feeds the family, pays the mortgage, and gets you invited to the dinner. The work channel is not optional. But output, on its own, is an unstable foundation for adult life. Output can stop. Output can be taken away. Output can become irrelevant when the industry shifts.

Output is contingent on conditions you do not fully control. A life organized around output is, in midlife, a life with a structural fragility you may not have noticed until the role ended.

The community channel produces *roots* — relationships, presence, repetition, place. Roots are different from output. Roots cannot be produced quickly. Roots require time. Roots require showing up at the same place, with the same people, on a regular cadence, without expecting anything to come of it. Roots are inefficient by every productivity metric. Roots are also what hold the rest of the structure up.

A life with output and no roots can be productive for a long time, and then collapse, suddenly, when the output stops. We have all seen this happen. The men we know who retired and were dead within three years had output without roots. The women we know who hit the empty nest and could not find their footing had output without roots. The founders we know who sold the company and disappeared into a depressed silence for two years had output without roots. The pattern is consistent enough to be diagnostic.

A life with roots and no output is also a problem, but it is a different and more recoverable kind of problem. The retirees who volunteer five days a week, run a Bible study, and play in a band on Saturday nights have roots without much output. They are, generally speaking, fine. They are not building anything that will outlast them economically, but they are not collapsing. The roots are doing what roots do.

The mature configuration is *both*. Output and roots. Work channel and community channel. Both are running in parallel. Each correcting for the other's failure modes.

This is what most readers of this book are missing and have not yet been told.

The wellness industry will sell you tools for the output channel — productivity, optimization, hustle, deep work, and focus. The wellness industry will not sell you tools for the community channel, because the community channel cannot be sold. The community channel must be *built*, in a specific local place, with specific local people, over the years. There is no app for that. There is no course that delivers it. There are no seven principles that will produce it within a calendar quarter.

I want to say a word about digital community, because most readers of this book have been told, for fifteen years, that they can have community online — and have not, despite trying, found that to be true.

An online community is not a community. An online community is *audience.* The two are not the same. Audience is the people who watch what you do; community is the people who would notice if you stopped. Audience is contingent on your continued performance; community is contingent on your continued presence. The audience does not require you to drive anywhere on a Saturday morning; the community does. Audience, when you are sick, does not bring you a casserole; the community does.

I am not saying the online community is worthless. I am saying it is structurally insufficient, by itself, as a foundation for the second channel of an adult life. The men and women I know who have tried to substitute online community for local community are, almost without exception, lonelier at sixty than they were at fifty. The men and women I know who have built a small local community — even a very small one, even a CPR class with eight people in it on the second Sunday of the month — are not. The pattern is consistent enough to be diagnostic.

Build the local thing. Use the online tools to support it if you want. But do not confuse the tools with the thing. The thing is the room with the people in it. The tools are scaffolding.

The community channel is built by *showing up* — at a youth sports field, at a library on the second Sunday of the month, at a Bible study on Wednesday nights, at a Habitat for Humanity build on Saturdays, at a local food pantry, at a small theater group, at a meditation circle, at a knitting club for new mothers, at the parking lot of a rec center where you have agreed to coach the third-grade basketball team.

The cadence is the practice.

The specific people are the membership.

The place is the place.

You build it the way the league was built and the way the CPR class was built and the way every other durable community institution in the history of communities has been built — by showing up, again, on a Saturday morning, when you do not particularly feel like it, because you said you would.

You may have three objections forming. Let me answer them now.

The first objection is: *I don't have time.* You probably have more time than you think. The community channel does not require much time per week. In its early years, the lacrosse league required four to six hours on a Saturday and an hour or two of administrative work midweek. Tom's CPR class is ninety minutes a month, plus a small amount of preparation. A reading group is two hours every other week. A youth coaching role is two practices and a game a week. None of these is a full-time commitment. None of these requires you to give up the work channel. The objection of "I don't have time" is, almost always, an objection about not having a *use* for the time, not an objection about the time itself. The chapter asks you to use a small portion of the time you currently have.

The second objection is: *community service feels like an obligation, not a relief.* That is because you have not yet found the right kind of community service. Bad community service feels like an obligation. Good community service does not. The difference is whether the service is *built* by you, in a specific room, with specific people, on a cadence that fits your life — versus *imposed* on you, by an organization, in a generic room, with generic people, on a cadence that does not. Most readers' bad experiences with community service have been imposed. The chapter is asking for the built kind.

The third objection is: *I am not the joiner type.* This is the rarest of the three objections, and the one that is most often used to avoid the chapter. *I am not the joiner type* is, in most cases, a self-description that has hardened over time into an identity claim. It is also, in most cases, not what the chapter is asking for. The chapter is not asking you to *join* anything. The chapter is asking you to *build* something. There is a meaningful difference between joining a community and building one. The first asks you to fit into someone else's structure. The second lets you create the structure. Most readers of this book are temperamentally better suited to the second than the first, and have been confusing the two because the only community options they have considered have been the joining kind.

The practice for this chapter is called the smallest thing worth building.

It works the same way the verbs-not-titles practice works, except it is aimed at the community channel rather than the work channel.

Take a piece of paper. (Same kind, plain, unlined or lined.)

At the top of the page, write the phrase *who passed something to me.* Below it, list the names of three to five people who, at some point in your life, passed forward something you still carry. A coach. A teacher. A neighbor. A grandmother. A mentor at your first job. A pastor. A scoutmaster. The man who ran the youth program at the YMCA when you were eleven. Be specific. Use first names. The names matter.

Next to each name, write the *thing* they passed. *Discipline. The habit of showing up. How to lose with grace. How to read a room. How to take care of someone smaller than you. How to ask a hard question. How to tell the truth when it costs you something.* Whatever your version is.

Now, somewhere on the page, write the question: *Where, locally, this week, can I pass forward what they passed to me?*

The question may not have a clean answer. That is fine. The question is the practice. Some readers, when they sit with the question for ninety minutes, will have an answer immediately. Others will need to sit with it for a week. A few will need to sit with it for a season. The sitting is the work; the answer will come in its own time.

When the answer comes, take *one small action* in its direction.

Not a grand commitment. Not a five-year plan to start a foundation. *One small action.* Send the email to the local school principal asking if they need a volunteer reader. Walk into the rec center and ask if they need a coach for the third-grade season. Call the hospital chaplain and ask whether they need someone to sit with patients on Tuesday afternoons. Send the message to the Boy Scout troop leader asking if they need a merit-badge counselor for the badge you happen to have spent thirty years performing the practice of.

The action is small. The action is specific. The action is the same kind of action you have been taking in every chapter of this book.

The community channel will be built, in the months and years that follow, on top of that one small action.

Save the page.

The reflection for this chapter is the smallest thing worth building practice in its most condensed form:

> *Name a coach, a mentor, a teacher, or a neighbor who, at some point in your life, passed something to you that you still carry. In two sentences, name what they passed. Then name one place — local, small, this week — where you could pass the same thing forward. Save the answer.*

You may discover, when you do this, that the place is closer than you think. Most readers do not have to invent the next room from scratch. Most readers find that the room is in a building they already drive past on Tuesdays — the rec center where their kids used to play, the library their wife uses, the YMCA two blocks from the office, the church they attend on holidays, the public school down the street whose principal would, in fact, be glad to hear from them.

The room is closer than you think.

The work is to walk in.

A note before we close.

You have just done two of the three channels. *Serve the work* and *serve the community.* The work channel produces output. The community channel produces roots. Together, they form the spine of a rebuilt adult life.

There is one channel left. It is the one most readers of this book will skip unless I insist they do not.

The third channel is *serve the future you.*

It is the channel almost no one takes seriously, because the future you is the only person on the obligation list who cannot, at this moment, complain. In the future, you cannot call me on Tuesday. In the future, you cannot show up at the apartment. The future you is the most patient of your obligations, and patience is precisely why the future you usually gets neglected.

The next chapter is about not neglecting them.

That is Chapter 9.

Chapter 9 — Serve the Future You

I want to tell you about the night I decided to start a Ph.D. program at forty-seven.

The decision was not, in the way decisions like this are presented in retrospect, dramatic. The decision was a slow accumulation that arrived, on a particular night, at a kind of obviousness I had not been ready for.

I was at home. The kids were older by then — past the age when bedtime routines had been the structure of our evenings. My wife was reading. I was sitting at the kitchen table with a mug of coffee that had gone cold, looking at the application materials for a doctoral program I had been thinking about, off and on, for the better part of two years.

I had not taken the application seriously until that night. I had been telling myself a story about why a man in his late forties, with a successful career, a stable family, a mortgage, and three channels of activity already running, would be insane to take on a doctoral program. The story had several plausible chapters. *I am too old. The work will not pay off in time. The professors will be ten years younger than me. The other students will be twenty years younger than me. The program will take five to seven years. By the time I finish, the value I can extract from the credential will be small.*

The story was correct in its facts.

The story was also, I noticed that night, not actually about the facts.

The story was about my unwillingness to commit to a thing whose returns would be primarily *internal* — to a man I was not yet, who would exist in fifteen or twenty years, and who I had been declining to invest in because the investment would not pay back in any economic sense within the time horizon I had been operating with.

I want to be precise about what I mean by *internal returns* because the chapter pivots on that precision.

I was not going to do a Ph.D. for a job. I did not pursue the Ph.D. for a salary bump. I was not going to do the Ph.D. for the credentials I needed in the workplace. I was not, in any sense, the productivity industry would recognize, going to do the Ph.D. for a *result*. I was going to do the Ph.D. because the man I wanted to be at sixty-five was, when I let myself imagine him, a man who had spent the last fifteen years of his life *deepening,* and I had no other structure available that would force the deepening to happen.

The deepening was the point.

The credential was, at most, a side effect.

And the version of me who would benefit, in the most direct sense, was not the version of me who would do the work. The version of me who would benefit was a version of me I did not know yet — the man who would exist after the doctorate, after the dissertation, after the thousand reading hours, after the conferences and the seminars and the late nights I was about to sign up for.

That man was, in the strict sense, a different person.

And the chapter you are reading is about him.

Or rather, it is about *your* version of him.

Here is the chapter's claim, said plainly:

The third channel of service in the rebuilt life is *the version of you who does not yet exist.*

The version of you who does not yet exist is the most patient of your obligations. They cannot call you on a Tuesday night. They cannot drive over on a Saturday morning. They cannot, in the daily logistics of your life, make any sound at all. They are the one obligation on your list that has no leverage. Their patience is the precise reason they are usually the obligation that gets neglected.

Most readers of this book have already neglected them.

That is not a moral charge. It is a description. The work channel and the community channel both make demands that are *immediate* — a brief, a Saturday morning, a phone call. The future-self channel does not make immediate demands. The future-self channel can be deferred indefinitely, without anyone noticing, including you. Most adults defer it indefinitely, and the deferral, accumulated over twenty years, produces the specific texture of midlife stuckness in which a person looks at themselves at fifty-five and notices that they have not, in any meaningful sense, *grown* in a decade.

That is what the future-self channel addresses.

The channel is built by committing — concretely, on a regular cadence, with no audience and no immediate payoff — to becoming a version of yourself that does not yet exist. The commitment is to a specific practice. The practice is sustained over the years. The years compound, in ways that are invisible at first and undeniable later, into a person who is not, at sixty-five, the person they would have been if they had skipped this channel.

That is the chapter you are reading.

Let me come back to the doctoral program, because the texture of the early years is the texture this chapter is asking you to be willing to sit with.

I started the program some months after the night at the kitchen table.

The first semester was the hardest I have had as a student. I had not been a full-time student in twenty-five years. The reading load was heavier than I remembered. The expectation that I could write at the level the program required was demonstrably wrong for the first three months. I could not write at that level. The professor of my first seminar, a woman younger than my younger sister, returned my first paper with comments that I had not, since my second year of college, been on the receiving end of. Her comments were correct. The paper was not good. I had not, in twenty years of writing for the squadron, Boeing, and various professional contexts, learned the kind of writing the program required.

I rewrote the paper. It was better. It was still not good. I rewrote it again.

That was the texture of the first semester. In reading, I was not yet good enough to engage at the expected level. In writing, I wasn't yet at the expected level. Discussions in seminars where younger students made connections that I had to think about for two days before I understood them. The accumulated experience of being, for the first time in two decades, the *least* qualified person in many of the rooms I was walking into.

I want to spend a moment on the embarrassment.

I had not anticipated the embarrassment, and the embarrassment was real, and most men in my position would not, I think, have stayed in the program past the point where the embarrassment became the dominant sensation of being there.

The embarrassment was not exactly the embarrassment of being old. The embarrassment was the embarrassment of being *visibly behind.* I had been senior in every professional context I had been part of for fifteen years. The role had been senior. The rank had been senior. The seniority was, in the slow way that seniority accumulates, baked into how I carried myself in rooms. The Ph.D. program did not care. The Ph.D. program asked me to be a beginner again, in front of younger people who were better at the work than I was, and the asking was not gentle.

There was a stretch in the second semester when I considered withdrawing.

I did not, at the time, articulate the consideration to my wife. I did not articulate it to the few friends who knew I was in the program. I articulated it to myself, late at night, with the same coffee that had gone cold at the kitchen table where I had decided to apply. The argument for withdrawal was strong. The argument went: *I am not getting better fast enough. The other students are running in circles around me. The professors are being polite, but they can see what I cannot do. I am embarrassing myself in a way I did not expect to, twenty years into a career. The credential will not pay off in any economic sense. I have a successful life. I do not need this.*

The argument was, on its facts, correct.

What pulled me through was not motivation. The motivation was thin. What pulled me through was the same thing that pulled me to brief at 0530 on a marginal pre-dawn morning twenty years earlier. *Obligation.* Specifically, an obligation to the man I had imagined that night at the kitchen table — the version of me at sixty-five who, when I let myself imagine him, was a man who had spent the last fifteen years deepening. That man was counting on me. He was the only person on my obligation list, in the entire program, who would notice if I dropped.

He noticed.

I stayed.

I want to tell you what happened by the third year, because that's the first year the channel started producing what it produces.

By the third year, I was no longer the worst writer in any seminar. By the third year, I had developed the reading discipline that the first semester had told me I lacked. By the third year, I had begun to think, in the middle of an ordinary Tuesday, in ways I had not been thinking before — connections between ideas, frames for problems I had been carrying for a decade, intellectual moves that the program had taught me by repetition over the course of a hundred seminar discussions. The man I had been imagining at the kitchen table was, in pieces, beginning to show up.

He was not finished. He is not finished now. I do not expect him to be finished by sixty-five. The program is a long arc, and the man at the end of it is just the beginning of a longer arc that will continue beyond my professional retirement.

But the channel was working.

The work was changing the worker.

That is what the third channel does, and that is why it is impossible to demonstrate to a reader on the front end. You cannot show someone what the channel will produce before they commit to it. You can only point to the men and women who have committed to similar channels, and to the visible difference between them and people who did not.

I want to point at one of those people now.

Aisha is forty-four. She works in a marketing role at a mid-sized tech company in a city where she did not grow up, and she lives there with her husband and three kids. Her marketing role is fine. Her family life is fine. Her commute is forty-five minutes, in a car, in traffic.

Three years ago, she started learning Arabic.

I want to be careful about the specifics, because they are the part most often misread. Aisha is not Arab by background. She has no professional reason to learn Arabic. She has no immediate family member who speaks it. She has no plans to live in an Arabic-speaking country. The Arabic was not, in any conventional sense, *useful.*

She started for a reason that, when she explains it, sounds slight in the telling and is not, in fact, slight at all.

A friend of hers, in college, had been from a family that spoke Arabic at home. The friend had, in some small way, she had not been able to fully articulate at the time, been *more herself* in Arabic than in English. Aisha had noticed, at twenty, that she envied the *more*. She had not, at the time, thought she could do anything about it. Twenty-two years later, she noticed that she still envied it, that no one was going to assign it to her, and that if she did not assign it to herself, she was going to die without ever becoming the person who could speak it.

She bought a $15 app and started using it on her Tuesday morning commute in March.

The first six months were terrible. Arabic is hard. The script is hard. The grammar is hard. The pronunciation is hard. She made progress at the rate that adult language learners make progress when they have forty-five minutes a day and a full life, which is to say, slow. She did not tell anyone. Her husband, who noticed the app on her phone, asked once. She said *just a thing I'm doing for me.* She did not elaborate. He let it go.

She has been in for three years.

She can read the script. She can hold a basic conversation. She is not fluent, by any standard. She is, in any measurable sense, still a beginner. But she has noticed, over the last six months, something that the apps, the books, and the pop culture would not have told her to expect.

The Arabic has changed her relationship to her own life.

She did not get a promotion because of her Arabic. She did not move to Beirut. She did not become a different person at work or in her marriage. What changed, when she let herself examine it, was something more interior. She had begun to think of herself as the kind of person who *commits to long arcs without an external payoff.* She had begun to think of herself as the kind of person who shows up to a thing for forty-five minutes a day, in a car, in traffic, on a Tuesday in March, when no one is asking her to. The forty-five minutes had been doing something. The doing had been changing the doer.

That is the third channel.

It is not visible. It does not produce a credential. In most cases, it does not produce a paycheck or a title. It produces a *person.* Specifically, it produces the version of the person who can do the kind of long-arc commitment the rest of life increasingly requires.

Aisha is forty-four. She has thirty more years of capacity ahead of her, on a normal expected trajectory, and the Arabic has set up a structural change in how she will spend them.

She did not start the Arabic for that reason. The reason emerged.

That is how the channel works.

I want to give you one more composite, because Aisha's situation is one in which the reader has cultural and family latitude to declare a private practice for herself. Many readers do not. Some come from cultures or families in which the very idea of *time set aside for the version of you who does not yet exist* reads as selfish.

Her name in this book is Amara. She is fifty-five. She came to the United States from Nigeria with her husband in her late twenties and worked as a registered nurse for twenty-five years, raising three children and supporting her mother and her husband's father across the long years their parents declined and died. She moved into a hospital-administration track three years ago, when her body began to tell her, the way bodies tell nurses past fifty, that the bedside work could not continue indefinitely.

The framework's first two channels did not surprise her. *Serve the work* was familiar. *Serve the community* was familiar; her church, her extended family, her neighborhood already required a substantial portion of her week, on a cadence that had been set when she was twenty-eight and had not changed since.

The future-self channel made her uncomfortable.

The discomfort had a specific shape. Inside the cultural frame she had been raised in, a fifty-five-year-old woman who *carved out an hour for herself* — to read, to study, to deepen — was a woman shirking obligations she should be honoring. Her mother, who had died at seventy-three, had not had a future-self practice. Her aunts had not. The notion that an hour of theology or piano was *owed to a version of herself in five years* was foreign to the obligation structure she had been living inside.

She set the framework down for two months while she sat with this.

What changed her mind was not an argument. It was a conversation with her oldest daughter, who is twenty-eight, who said something offhand about her mother *sounding tired in a way she had not always sounded.* Amara heard the comment differently than her daughter intended. She heard it as a description of a woman who was running on three other people's obligations and not maintaining the engine that produced the woman herself.

She started the future-self channel that week. The practice she chose was reading — specifically, a long arc of theology she had wanted to engage with for thirty years and had never had the language to claim time for. Forty-five minutes, four mornings a week, before anyone else in the house was awake.

She has been at it for eight months. The practice has changed the practitioner. The morning hour is the only hour of her week that she does not justify to anyone, and the not-justifying is, she has begun to suspect, what the channel is actually for.

The cultural complication is real. The framework still works inside it. The argument the chapter has been making — that the future-self channel is the most generous of the three because it builds the version of you others will eventually depend on — is the argument that, eventually, gave Amara permission to take the hour.

You may need the same permission. The chapter is giving it to you.

____

Let me say what is happening, mechanically, when serving the future you works.

The future-self channel is the channel almost no one takes seriously, and the channel that, when it is sustained, produces the largest compounding effect of any of the three.

The reason no one takes it seriously is that the future self has no leverage. The work channel can hold you accountable through your paycheck. The community channel can hold you accountable through the people who show up next to you on the field. The future-self channel can only hold you accountable through *you* — the present version of you, choosing to honor an obligation to a person who does not yet exist and cannot enforce the obligation in any external way.

That is, structurally, an unstable arrangement.

Most adults, when faced with an unstable arrangement, defer it. They defer the future-self investment. They defer the long arc. They defer the practice that has no audience. They tell themselves they will get to it when the kids are older, when the work calms down, when the next promotion arrives, when the renovation is finished, when the parents are settled, when the season changes. The deferrals are not unreasonable in the short term. The deferrals, in aggregate, over twenty years, produce the specific kind of midlife stuckness in which a person looks at the calendar of their last decade and notices that nothing in it represents *growth into* anyone. They are the same person they were ten years ago. They are simply older.

The future-self channel is the only thing that prevents that.

The way the channel works is by binding you, in the present, to a person who does not yet exist, on a regular cadence, in a specific practice, for a long enough stretch that the practice begins to deposit on you the qualities of the future person.

The deposit is not theoretical. It is structural.

If you read in a discipline for an hour a day, for ten years, you are a person who has read in that discipline for ten years. You are a different person from the one who did not. The ten years are non-negotiable. The hour is non-negotiable. The compounding cannot be bought. The compounding cannot be hacked. The compounding can only be done.

Most adults do not do it.

To be clear, the channel is not about productivity.* The channel is about *becoming*. The work channel is, at its best, about becoming. But the work channel is also constrained by what the role requires of you, and the role does not always require you to become anyone in particular. The future-self channel is unconstrained. The future-self channel is the place where you, alone, decide who you are going to spend the next ten years becoming, and then make the small daily commitment that produces it.

The making of that commitment is the practice.

The practice is the channel.

Some readers, when they reach this point in the chapter, will immediately know what their future self practice is. They have been carrying it for years — a half-finished novel, a discontinued musical instrument, a degree they almost completed, a craft they once apprenticed in, a body of work they have been meaning to read since college. For these readers, the chapter's practical move is simple: commit to the thing you already know is yours. The not-doing is, at this point, the only thing standing between you and the channel.

A larger group of readers will not, on first reading, know what their future selves' practice should be. They have several candidate practices, but none of them feels obviously *the* one. They are afraid of choosing wrong.

To these readers, I want to say: choose anyway.

The practice you choose at forty-five does not have to be the only practice you ever commit to. It does not have to be the right practice.

It needs to be *a* practice — a serious, sustained, long-arc practice that will deposit something on you over the next five years. If you discover, in year three, that the practice was not the right one, you will be a different person than the person who started, and the discovery itself will be a kind of deposit. The work was not wasted. The work was building the practitioner.

The fear of choosing wrong is the form the deferral takes. The deferral, repeated for ten years, is the actual loss. Not the choosing. The not-choosing.

Pick something. Start. The first hour is more important than the first hour being correct.

I want to tell you what most adults reach for when they are looking for the future-self channel and do not yet have language for it. They reach for *bucket lists.* The bucket list is the wellness industry's version of the future-self channel, and the bucket list is wrong about the channel in the same way the find-your-passion advice is wrong about the work channel.

The bucket list is item-based. *I want to climb Kilimanjaro. I want to write a novel. I want to learn to play the cello. I want to see the Northern Lights.* The bucket list assumes the future-self channel is composed of a list of *experiences* the person will accumulate. The list is, on examination, mostly *consumption.* The experiences are good experiences; the consumption of them is not, in itself, the channel.

The future-self channel is composed of *practices,* not experiences.

A practice is something you do on a regular cadence that changes who you are. Reading is a practice. Studying a language is a practice. Training for a marathon is a practice. Learning to play an instrument is a practice. Apprenticing to a craft is a practice. Sitting with a teacher in a tradition is a practice. The practices have a long arc. The arc deposits something on you. The deposit is the channel.

The bucket list does not deposit anything. The bucket list is a record of consumption. Consumption is fine; consumption is not the channel.

If you are choosing your future self investment, choose a practice. Not a list of things to consume.

That is the engine of the chapter.

––––––––––

You may have three objections forming. Let me answer them now.

The first objection is: *I am too old.* You are not too old. There is no age at which the future self channel stops working, because the future self exists at every age. The eighty-year-old who starts learning piano is not foolish. The eighty-year-old has a future self at eighty-five who will have been playing piano for five years, instead of a person who has not been. The math works at every age. The math has only ever stopped working for people who are dying within the year, and even then, it sometimes still works. The "too old" objection is a misapplication of a productivity calculation to a non-productivity domain. The channel is not about return on investment in the economic sense. The channel is about who you become.

The second objection is: *it won't pay off in time.* The "in time" framing is the framing the work channel uses, and the framing is wrong here. The future-self channel is not paying off the way the work channel pays off. The future-self channel is gradually depositing into the person you are becoming. There is no "time" by which the deposit must arrive in order to count. The deposit accumulates as long as the practice continues. The deposit is the practice. There is no other deliverable.

The third objection is: *this feels selfish given everyone else who needs me.* This is the one I want to push back on hardest. The future-self channel is not selfish. It is the most generous of the three channels because the version of you it produces is the one the people in the other two channels will eventually depend on. The you at sixty-five who has spent fifteen years deepening will be more useful to your wife, your children, your grandchildren, your colleagues, and your community than the you at sixty-five who skipped the channel. The skipping is not generosity. The skipping is, often, a form of avoidance dressed in the costume of duty. The channel is the cure for the avoidance. The channel is, finally, what makes you a person worth being depended on.

The practice for this chapter is called *the future-self commitment.*
Take a piece of paper.
At the top of the page, write *the version of me at five years from now.*
Now describe that person. Not in a list. In a paragraph. Be specific. *They read in a discipline I do not currently know. They speak a language I do not currently speak. They have a craft they have been practicing for five years. They train in a physical practice I do not currently train in. They have read the great books I have not yet read. They write the kind of writing I currently cannot.* Pick the version of yourself you have been quietly imagining and have not been giving permission to invest in.
Now underline the verbs.
Pick one of the underlined verbs. The smallest and most concrete one. Not the most ambitious one — the most concrete one. *Reads. Writes. Practices. Studies. Trains. Apprentices. Sits with a teacher.*
Schedule the first hour this week on the calendar.
The first hour is the practice. The first hour is the rep. You do not have to know what hour two looks like. You do not have to commit to the long arc on day one. You commit to the first hour. After the first hour, you commit to the second hour on the calendar for the next week. Then the third. The arc builds itself one hour at a time, the same way the work channel and the community channel build themselves one hour at a time.
Three rules.
The first rule: *do not tell anyone for the first thirty days.* The future-self channel is the only one of the three that does best in private. Telling people about it, before the practice has roots, weakens the

practice. People will react. People will encourage. People will ask you about it on day three. The asking will translate into a *performance* of the practice rather than the practice itself. Keep it private until it is a habit. Then you can tell whoever you want.

The second rule: *protect the cadence.* The cadence — once a week, twice a week, a particular hour at a particular time — is more important than the volume. A consistent hour a week for ten years is a different person at the end. A wildly variable five hours a week for two years and zero hours a week for eight is the same person you started with. The cadence is the channel.

The third rule: *do not try to optimize.* Most readers of this book have spent thirty years in environments that rewarded optimization. The future-self channel does not. The future-self channel rewards *showing up,* not optimizing the showing up. The optimizing is, in practice, a sophisticated form of avoidance. Resist it.

Save the page.

The reflection for this chapter is the future-self commitment in its most condensed form:

> *Write a one-paragraph description of yourself five years from now. Make it specific: what they read, what they can do, what they have been practicing. Underline the verbs. Pick one. Book the first hour this week on your calendar. Don't tell anyone for thirty days. Save the page.*

You may discover, when you do this, that the version of you in five years has been waiting for this assignment for a long time. Most readers of this book, when they let themselves describe the person without filtering, find that the person is already legible — already named — and has been quietly waiting for you to commit to becoming them. The commitment is the chapter you are reading.

Save the page.

A note before we go on.

You have just done all three channels. *Serve the work. Serve the community. Serve the future you.* Each channel produces something the others cannot produce. Each channel, run alone, eventually fails. Each channel, run together with the other two, produces a life with the structural integrity of a tripod.

The next chapter is about the tripod.

Specifically, it is about how to run all three at once, what to do when one of them is starving, and how to use the lowest-scoring channel as the diagnostic for where this week's hour belongs.

That is Chapter 10.

Chapter 10 — Running the Three Together

I want to tell you about a stretch of months in my late forties when something quietly remarkable happened, and I did not, while it was happening, recognize it.

By that point, I was running all three channels.

I was at Boeing. The work was real, and the duty was clear. I was running the lacrosse league. The community was real, and the Saturdays were structured. I was several years into the doctoral program. The future-self channel was what I was doing in private on weeknights, with a stack of books on the kitchen table after the kids had gone to bed.

The three channels did not, on most weeks, feel related. The channels lived in different parts of my life. The work channel had its own calendar, its own people, its own rooms. The community channel had its own. The future-self channel had its own. Each had its own logic. Each had its own demands. I was running all three the way a person runs three separate apps on a phone.

What I want to tell you about is the stretch when I noticed the apps had begun talking to each other.

I don't have the exact week the noticing started. The realization is the kind that accumulates and then shows up, on a Tuesday afternoon, fully formed. The Tuesday I noticed went something like this: I was in a meeting at Boeing, listening to a presentation about a system upgrade and a stakeholder-management problem the program was trying to solve. The problem was, as so many problems in defense programs are, not technical but human — a question of how to align several groups of people with different incentives toward a common outcome. The presenter was sketching the dynamics on a whiteboard.

I noticed, while watching the whiteboard, that the dynamics on it were the same ones I had been thinking about for the league.

The league had its own version of stakeholder management. Parents, coaches, refs, the parks department, the sponsors — each with its own incentives, its own short-term and long-term interests, its own friction points with the others. I had been managing those tensions for years, intuitively, on Saturday mornings, in folding chairs, with coffee. The thing the Boeing presenter was sketching at the whiteboard was, structurally, the same thing.

I had not noticed the parallel before that afternoon.

And then I noticed something else, which is that the way I had been thinking about the league dynamics was, in turn, shaped by a paper I had read for the doctoral program two months earlier — a paper about coordination problems in organizations that had given me a vocabulary I had not previously had for what I had been doing on Saturdays.

The Boeing meeting was, in a small way, being conducted with a vocabulary I had picked up in the doctoral program, in service of a problem that had its analog in the lacrosse league.

The three channels were no longer three.

That was the noticing. That is the chapter you are reading.

Here is the chapter's claim, said plainly:

The three channels are not a menu. They are a system.

When you run them as a menu — picking the one you happen to feel like working on this week, ignoring the others, running on whichever is currently producing the most visible output — you get less from each of them than you would if you ran them together. The reason is structural. Each channel, on its own, develops a kind of *insularity.* The work channel develops the insularity of professionalism. The community channel develops the insularity of localism. The future-self channel develops the insularity of self-reference. Each insularity has its own pathologies, and each is corrected, almost automatically, by the active presence of the other two.

A man who runs only the work channel is a man whose entire framework for understanding life is the one his profession provides. A man who runs only the community channel is a man whose entire framework is that of his town. A man running only the future-self channel is a man whose entire framework is the framework of his own private practice. Each framework, alone, is partial. Each framework, in conversation with the other two, becomes more honest than any of them could be in isolation.

Running the three together produces something none of them can produce alone: cross-pollination.* The lessons of one channel inform the others. The blindness of one channel is corrected by the others. The version of you that emerges from running all three is, structurally, a more complete version than any single-channel life can produce.

That is the engine of this chapter.

———————————

I want to give you more examples of the cross-pollination, because the examples are the point. The examples are how you recognize the system once it starts working.

The example I gave you above ran from the work channel back through the community channel, through the future-self channel, and into the work channel again, in a single Tuesday afternoon. There were others.

I noticed, in the second year of running the league, that the rhythm of a Saturday — the structure of a coaching session, the specific cadence of teaching a complex skill to an eight-year-old, the compression of a pre-game brief into ninety seconds for kids who were not going to absorb anything longer — was teaching me something about teaching that I had not previously known. As a result, the Boeing meetings became sharper. I noticed that I was structuring presentations differently. I was opening with the thing the audience needed to know in the first thirty seconds, the way a youth coach opens with the one thing the kids need to remember when the game starts. The lacrosse field had retrained me as a presenter. I had not noticed it had done so until the Boeing meetings began to go differently.

I noticed, in the third year of the doctoral program, that the discipline of writing in an academic register was teaching me something about writing in any register. The things the professors had been correcting in my papers — vagueness, abstraction, hedging, the use of large words where small ones would do — were the same things that, on examination, had been weakening my work emails for years. The doctoral program had retrained me as a writer. The retrained writer was a better writer at Boeing, too. I had not, before the program, recognized that my workplace writing was generating the same kinds of imprecision the professors were marking up in my seminar papers.

I noticed, in the fourth year of running the league, that the quality of attention required to run a youth practice — the specific kind of presence required to hold the focus of fifteen ten-year-olds for ninety minutes in late-afternoon heat — was a kind of attention that, when I let it, made me better at the doctoral program. As a result, the seminars became different. I was more present in them. I was listening more carefully. The lacrosse field had retrained me as a student.

Each channel taught me something that none of the others would have taught me on its own.

The cross-pollination was not, however, automatic. I had to be willing to let the channels speak to each other, and the willingness was a posture I had to develop. Most adults running three things in parallel run them as three separate things. They keep them in separate compartments. The compartments are useful — they prevent the work channel from leaking into the community channel in unhelpful ways — but the compartments also block the cross-pollination that is the system's most valuable output.

The way you let the channels speak to each other is by *noticing*. You notice, in the middle of a Boeing meeting, that the problem on the whiteboard is the problem on the lacrosse field. You notice, while reading a paper at the kitchen table, that the argument is one you have been making, in less precise terms, in conference calls for years. You notice, while running a Saturday practice, that the way you are explaining a defensive concept to ten-year-olds is teaching you something about how to explain a complex idea to a senior executive on Monday. The noticing is the practice. The noticing makes the cross-pollination available.

I want to tell you, briefly, about the year all three channels overlapped most fully.

This was the second year of the doctoral program, the third year of running the league, and a year at Boeing in which I had moved into a role with more strategic latitude than before. The three were running at high intensity simultaneously. The schedule was tight. My wife was patiently watching me run the schedule and saying nothing. She was reading me. She was doing a long-term assessment of whether the schedule was sustainable.

What I noticed, that year, was that the schedule was not, structurally, the problem. The schedule was tight, but it was integrated. The hours did not feel like three competing demands. The hours felt like three legs of the same instrument. When I did the work well, the league was easier. When I did well in the league, the seminars were easier. When I did well in the seminars, the work was easier. The integration was the system. The system was more than the sum of its parts.

I am writing this many years later, and the three channels are still running. The work channel has changed shape. The league has matured. The doctoral program has become a different kind of practice in the years since I finished. But the three are still running, together, the way they have been running for almost two decades. And the running of them together is, more than anything else, what I would point to if you asked me how a man my age stays in motion.

The three together are the answer.

The three apart is the half-answer most adults are running on, and the reason most adults of my generation are visibly tired even when they have nothing in particular to be tired about.

Let me give you a civilian version of what happens when one channel is starving the other two.

The version I want to give you is composite — drawn from several conversations I have had with several readers of an earlier version of this material — but the texture is consistent enough across those conversations that the composite reads as honest.

Her name in this book is Janelle. She is fifty-two. She is a senior executive at a privately held company in a midsize city. She has, by every external measure, done well. In her case, the work channel is producing. The output is real. The compensation is good. The work, on its terms, is meaningful.

She came to the framework looking for help with the stuckness she could not name.

She had read the book. She had done the exercises. She had identified the duty in her previous role and was intentionally running the work channel. By month three of her own engagement with the framework, the work channel was clearly the strongest of her three. The work channel, in fact, was the *only* one of her three.

Over the previous decade, she had allowed the community channel to thin out. She had not built anything local. Her social life consisted of her marriage, which was in its third decade, functional but not particularly attended to, and a small set of friends she texted about once a quarter. Her town, in any meaningful sense, did not know her.

She had, over the same decade, allowed the future-self channel to thin out completely. She had no practice. She read in her field, which was a work-channel investment dressed in future-self clothing, but she did not read outside her field. She had no creative practice. She had no physical practice past the obligatory three-day-a-week gym routine that did not, in any structural sense, deposit anything on her. The future-self channel, upon inspection, had a score of approximately 1 out of 10.

The result, when she audited it, was a person who was producing impressively in one channel and starving in the other two.

I'll tell you what was happening, structurally, when she audited.

The work channel, on its own, was producing the texture of her life. The texture was: working a lot. Sleeping less than she should. Drinking a glass of wine in the evening, which had recently become two. Having difficulty being present with her husband on weekends. Feeling, on Sunday nights, the kind of background dread that is the standard signal of a life over-rotated to one channel.

The fix was not to add more work-channel optimization. The fix was to feed the other two.

After the audit, she started with the community channel. She walked into the local literacy center on a Tuesday afternoon and asked if they needed a volunteer reader. They did. She started showing up for an hour on Tuesday afternoons. Tuesday afternoon was, in the first weeks, a struggle to protect from the work channel, which kept trying to colonize it. The community channel held. By month three, the Tuesday hour had become non-negotiable.

She started, simultaneously, with the future-self channel. She picked up a guitar she had played in college and had not touched in twenty-five years. She did not announce this to anyone. She practiced for thirty minutes, three nights a week, after her husband had gone to bed.

By month six, the work channel was, paradoxically, producing better than it had been. The dread was gone. The wine had returned to one glass. The marriage, without any direct intervention, had become more honest. The community channel and the future-self channel, when fed, were doing what they were designed to do: correcting the failure modes of running on the work channel alone.

This is what running the three together does.

Let me say what is happening, mechanically, when running the three together works.

The integration produces three structural effects that none of the channels produces on its own.

The first effect is *correction*. Each channel, run in isolation, develops blindness that the other two would have caught. The work channel, alone, does not notice when it has crowded out everything else. The community channel, alone, does not notice when it has become a substitute for personal growth. The future-self channel, alone, does not notice when it has become a sophisticated form of solipsism. The presence of the other two channels is the corrective. The other two channels are, in effect, the sanity check on the one you are most over-investing in.

The second effect is *cross-pollination,* which we have already discussed. The lessons of one channel become available to the others. The frame from the work channel becomes useful in the community channel. The discipline from the community channel becomes useful in the future-self channel. The patience from the future-self channel becomes useful in the work channel. Each channel is, when running, a kind of school. The schools are different. The lessons each one teaches you are different. Running all three means being a student at three different schools simultaneously, and that simultaneity produces a kind of education that no single school can provide.

The third effect is *resilience.* This one is the most important and the least visible. When you run all three channels, you have three load-bearing structures holding you up at any given time. If one of them fails — and one of them will, eventually, fail; that is the nature of channels — the other two are still there. A man who has only the work channel and loses his job has lost everything. A man who has only the community channel and moves to a new town has lost everything. A man who has only the future-self channel and develops a chronic health problem has lost everything. A man who is running all three has lost a third. The other two-thirds is nothing. The other two-thirds is, in most cases, what carries him through the season of the failed channel.

I want to be specific about this last point because it is the structural reason this book exists in the form it does.

Most readers of this book are reading it because *one channel has just failed.* The role ended. The kids left. The marriage shifted. The role of caretaker for an aging parent is over. Whatever the channel was, it has ended. The reader is at the kitchen counter at 5:47 a.m., looking at the cavity it left. That is most of you.

The reason a person in that position can rebuild is that there were always two other channels available, even when the failed channel was dominant. Even if you have not been running them, they are there. The work channel can be re-engaged. The community channel can be built. The future-self channel can be started. The book has been, in a sense, an extended argument for the obviousness of this — that even when one channel has ended, two more are available, and that the two more are the place where the rebuild happens.

A reader running all three before the failure recovers faster. A reader who started running all three after the failure recovers a little slower but recovers nonetheless. Either way, the structure of the recovery is the same. You feed the channels that are still available. The fed channels carry the load while the failed channel either heals or is replaced.

This is what every meaningful adult life with any kind of re-silience has been built on, whether or not the people inside those lives have ever named it that way.

You have just named it.

The naming is the work of the chapter.

You may have three objections forming. Let me answer them now.

The first objection is: *running three things at once feels like a lot.* It is. I am not pretending otherwise. The three together make for a tighter schedule than running them one at a time. But the three together are also a *more sustainable* schedule than running one at a time, for the structural reasons we just covered. The three together produce less week-to-week intensity than the one-channel-at-a-time pattern most adults run, because they do not require any one channel to carry the entire load. A reader with three channels at moderate intensity is, on most weeks, less tired than a reader with one channel at high intensity. The math is not intuitive. The math is correct.

The second objection is: *can't I run them sequentially? Get the work channel established, then add the community, then add the future-self?* You can. Some readers do. The sequential approach is slower but works for some personality types. The risk is that the channel you start with becomes the one you overinvest in, and the others never get added because the first one absorbs all available capacity. Most readers who go sequentially never get to channels two and three. Most readers who go simultaneously get to all three within twelve months. I am recommending simultaneous, but I will not argue with sequential if it is the only configuration you can make work.

The third objection is: *what if I am only good at one of the three?* You will be. Most people are. The chapter is not asking you to be equally good at all three. The chapter is asking you to *run* all three. The "good at" framing is a residue of the work channel's logic, where being good at something is the metric. The community channel and the future-self channel are not measured by how good you are at them. They are measured by whether you are *in* them. You can be a mediocre coach and still run the community channel. You can be a slow language learner and still run the future-self channel. Mediocre channels, run consistently, deliver everything the chapter is promising. The good at framing is, in this context, a form of avoidance. Drop it.

The practice for this chapter is called the Sunday audit.

It is a five-minute practice. It is the only practice in the book that runs weekly, indefinitely, for the rest of your life.

On Sunday morning — or Sunday afternoon, or Sunday evening; the specific time matters less than the consistency of doing it on Sundays — take a piece of paper. (You know the paper by now. Plain. Unlined or lined. Same kind you have been using.)

Write three column headings at the top of the page:

Work. Community. Future you.

Underneath each heading, score yourself on a scale of one to ten for the past week. The score is not based on hours invested. The score is based on whether you, in your own honest assessment, met your version of the channel for the week.

The work channel score is high if the work you did this week honored the duty under the title. Low if you went through the motions on the role and did not bring yourself to it.

The community channel score is high if you showed up at the place where you have agreed to be useful, were present, and were reliable. Low if the community-channel commitment slid this week, or if you have not yet built one.

The future-you channel score is high if you maintained your practice this week — the hour, the cadence, the commitment. Low if you skipped, or if the practice has not yet been chosen.

You are not averaging the three. The average is irrelevant. What you are looking at, when you have the three numbers in front of you, is the *lowest* score.

The lowest score is where this week's hour belongs.

That is the entire diagnostic. The chapter has spent four thousand words leading up to it.

If the lowest is the work channel, this week's hour is a one-hour meeting with the duty under your old or current role. If the lowest is the community channel, this week's hour is a one-hour show-up at the local place where you have agreed to be useful. If the lowest is the future-self channel, this week's hour is one of the practice sessions you have been postponing.

You do not have to fix the lowest channel this week. You have to put one hour against it.

Then you write the date at the top of the page. You file it. (A folder marked *Sunday audits* is enough; nothing fancy.) You repeat next Sunday.

To make this concrete, a representative Sunday audit might look something like this:

Work — 7. Showed up. Made the call I had been putting off about the contract. Wrote the section of the proposal that mattered most. Did not, however, do the deeper work I had been planning on the strategy memo.

Community — 4. Went to the Saturday practice but was distracted. Did not call back the parent who emailed about the equipment fund. Did not make the Wednesday meeting at church — sent regrets.

Future you — 2. Skipped the practice on four of seven nights. Did the practice on Tuesday and Friday, but the cadence broke.

The lowest is the future-self channel at 2. This week's hour is in the future-self channel. Specifically: the practice, three nights this week, no exceptions, and a calendar block on Sunday afternoon to make sure the cadence does not break a second week.

That is the entire audit. Five minutes. Three numbers. One decision about where the hour goes. File the page. Repeat next Sunday.

I want to acknowledge how small that sounds. The smallness is the design. Most adults who try to do something larger on a Sunday — a long journaling practice, a quarterly review, a strategic planning session — quietly stop within three weeks. The five-minute audit survives the years. Some readers do this with a cup of coffee at the kitchen counter. Some do it on a porch in the morning. Some do it on a pew on the way out of church. The setting does not matter. The five minutes does.

By the end of the year, you will have fifty-two Sunday audits. The audits will be a record, in your own handwriting, of where the three channels have been each week of the year. You will notice patterns. You will notice the months when one channel was starving. You will notice the months when the integration was working. The audits will, over time, become the most accurate dashboard you have ever had on whether you are, in any structural sense, in motion.

A note about seasons.

There will be seasons in which one channel must, of necessity, dominate. A new baby. A health crisis. A parent in their last weeks. A startup at the moment of acquisition. A degree program in its final year. These seasons are real, and the chapter is not asking you to maintain a clean three-way balance through them.

What the chapter is asking is that, even in the dominant-channel seasons, you do not let the other two go to zero. A single hour a week in the community channel is not balanced, but it is not zero either. A thirty-minute future-self practice on Saturday morning, when the rest of the week has been the new baby or the health crisis, is not balanced, but it is also not zero. The Sunday audit, in those seasons, is doing maintenance on the channels you cannot fully run, so that when the season ends, the channels are still there to be returned to.

This is the structural reason the audit is weekly rather than monthly. A monthly audit can survive a long stretch of imbalance without registering it. A weekly audit cannot. The weekly audit is, in effect, a check that the dominant-channel season is not silently dismantling the other two.

When the season ends — and the seasons end — the audit is what makes the return possible. The return is the practice.

The reflection for this chapter is the Sunday audit in its first rep:

On a piece of paper, write three column headings: Work. Community. Future you. Score yourself one to ten on each for the past week. Don't average. Look at the lowest score. Pick a thirty-minute action for the lowest channel. Take it before next Sunday. File the page. Repeat next Sunday.

You will, in the first few weeks of running this practice, learn things about your three channels that you did not know. You will discover that one of them has been running on autopilot for months. You will discover that another has been receiving most of your attention without producing much. You will discover that the channel you thought was your strong suit is, on examination, the channel that has been silently starving. Over time, the audits will show you what the channels are actually doing, rather than what you have been assuming they are doing.

That information is the diagnosis. The information lets you adjust. The adjustment, run weekly for years, produces the integrated three-channel life that this chapter has been describing.

That is the engine. That is, finally, the system.

A note before we close.

You have just been given the entire architecture of the rebuilt life.

Three channels. The next right step practice that holds them together day to day. The Sunday audit that holds them together week to week. Obligation is the engine of all of it.

That is the system.

The system is yours now.

The remaining chapters of the book are not about adding to the system. They are about *staying in* the system through the long, unromantic stretches when the system does not produce visible results — and the slightly different question of what, in the end, the system is producing.

The next chapter is the honest one about the long middle.

That is Chapter 11.

Chapter 11 — When It Doesn't Feel Like Progress

I want to tell you about an eighteen-month stretch in my life when nothing was working.

I want to be careful with the language. *Nothing was working* is not the same thing as *everything was failing.* The work was not failing. The league was not failing. The doctoral program was not failing. By any external measurement, all three of my channels were running. The hours were being put in. The cards were being written and worked. The Sundays were being audited. The system was, in the most literal sense, operating.

What was missing was the *output.* The thing every one of those channels had produced, in the past, when it was running well — a sense of forward motion, a sense of being on the arc, a sense of becoming somebody — was, for eighteen months, gone.

The Boeing year was a slow one. I was assigned to a program that was, for reasons I will not bore you with, mired in administrative paralysis. The decisions I was making were being undone by decisions made in other meetings I was not invited to. The work was real, but it was producing nothing visible. I was working hard most weeks and accomplishing very little.

The league had had a difficult season. A coach had quit in the middle of the year. A parent had filed a complaint about something that, when investigated, turned out to be a misunderstanding, and the parent never quite stopped being upset about it. Two of the kids who had been in the program from the beginning had aged out, and I had not, before they left, had the kind of conversation with them that I had imagined I would. The season had ended without incident, but without joy.

The dissertation was a wall.

I had been writing the same chapter for six months. The chapter was not getting better. My adviser, a careful woman who did not say more than was necessary, had read the third revision and had returned it with a note that I could only describe as *patient.* Her patience was, on examination, the most damning thing she could have given me. I was not making the kind of progress a third-revision draft is supposed to make. I knew it. She knew it. The chapter knew it.

This is what eighteen months of *nothing visible* feels like.

I want to tell you what kept me in motion through that stretch, and what did not.

What did not keep me in motion was inspiration. The inspiration was offline for the entire eighteen months. There was no meaningful day in that period when I felt the particular sensation that the wellness industry calls being *on fire about my work.* I was on fire about nothing. I was, on most days, going through the motions of a life I had built with intention, and noticing that the motions were producing nothing in particular, and continuing to perform them anyway.

What kept me in motion was the system.

The next-right-step rule kept me writing the index card every night. The Sunday audit kept me looking at the three channels every week. The obligation engine kept me showing up — at Boeing, at the field, at the desk with the dissertation — because there were specific people on the other end of each commitment whose lives would be different if I stopped.

The system did not produce any visible result for eighteen months.

The system also did not let me stop.

That is the chapter you are reading.

———————————————

Here is the chapter's claim, said plainly:

Most of the time you spend on a meaningful adult life will not feel like progress.

I want to give that sentence room.

Most of the time. Not some of the time. Not the bad weeks. Most of it. The default texture of a life organized around the work channel, the community channel, and the future-self channel is not the texture of forward motion. The default texture is repetition. Showing up. Doing the work. Filling the cards. Running the audits. Watching nothing in particular happen for stretches that, by their measure, are longer than any reasonable person would think necessary.

The reason this is so is structural. The channels produce results on a long arc. The arc is years, not weeks. A year of careful Boeing work produces a result that shows up two years later in a system upgrade, and nobody traces it back to the year of work. A season of careful coaching produces a result that shows up four years later, when the kid who was eight is now twelve and is the kind of player a particular kind of coach produces. A year of dissertation reading produces a result that shows up in a paragraph in a chapter in a book you write five years later.

The arc is real. The arc is invisible from inside the year you are in.

And the year you are in is where most of your life will be lived.

The chapter asks you to be honest with yourself about that, because the readers who quit the system are almost always the ones who could not tolerate the eighteen months during which the system did not, by their measure, produce.

You cannot make the eighteen months shorter. You can, however, learn to read them honestly.

That is the chapter you are reading.

———————————————

I want to come back to the eighteen-month stretch because I want to be precise about what it actually felt like to live through and what got me through.

The Boeing year first. I want to describe a Tuesday in the middle of that year, because the Tuesday is more useful than the year.

I had a meeting at 10 a.m. with three other people about a piece of the program I had been working on for some months. The meeting had been scheduled, postponed, scheduled, postponed, and finally held — and at the meeting, after thirty minutes of discussion, we agreed on a path forward that I, at the time, believed was the right path. I left the meeting somewhat encouraged. By Friday of that same week, the path forward had been quietly killed by a decision from a different meeting I had not been part of, made on considerations that had nothing to do with the technical merit of what we had agreed to. I learned about the killing through a forwarded email. I sat at my desk reading the email for some minutes. I did not know whether to be angry or amused. I settled on neither and went back to work.

That kind of week happened, on average, once a month during the year.

Most of my work was being eaten, in the small ways that work in large organizations gets eaten, by considerations that had nothing to do with whether the work was good. There was no satisfying response to this. There was no productivity hack that would have made the work less subject to the considerations. The considerations were the system in which I was working. The work continued. The work continued because it was a duty and because there were people on the other end who would eventually benefit, even if no individual week of the year I was in showed any visible benefit at all.

That is the work channel during eighteen months of nothing visible.

The league was different in texture but identical in shape. I want to describe a Saturday in October of the difficult season, because the Saturday is the most useful thing I can tell you.

Saturday was rainy. We had three games scheduled. Two were canceled. The third went ahead on a field that was, by the second quarter, a mud pit. The kids were unhappy. The parents were unhappy. The refs were trying to keep the games safe in conditions that were, at best, marginally safe. A coach yelled at me on the sideline about the scheduling. The yelling was mostly about other things in the coach's life, but the yelling was directed at me, and I was the natural recipient of it because I had been the one running the league for some years, and I had, in some sense, signed up for being yelled at on muddy Saturdays in October.

I drove home that afternoon with the wettest pair of sneakers I had owned in years and the kind of hollow tiredness that does not come from physical exertion. The league was not, that day, producing the thing I had built it to produce. The league was producing complaints, weather problems, and one coach who needed to vent about his own life.

The system kept me in the league. The system did not pretend the day had been good. The system simply did not let me decide, based on the day, that the league was not worth running.

The dissertation was the hardest of the three.

I want to describe a particular evening, in February of the worst stretch, at my home desk, with a draft of the chapter open on the screen and a half-empty cup of coffee that had gone cold three hours earlier. I had been writing the same paragraph for forty minutes. The paragraph was not getting better. I was, by any reasonable measure, not making progress on the chapter, the dissertation, or the project of becoming a man who could write at the level the program required.

I closed the laptop at 11:47 p.m.

I wrote on the index card on my desk: *spend forty-five minutes tomorrow on the chapter. Same paragraph. No new section. Just the paragraph.*

I did exactly what the card said the next morning. I spent forty-five minutes. The paragraph did not improve appreciably. I wrote the next card.

I want you to hold that scene for a moment, because that scene is the chapter.

That is what most of the work, during the long stretches when it is not working, looks like. It does not look like inspiration. It does not look like a breakthrough. It does not look like the slow climbing of a known mountain. It looks like a man at a desk, with a paragraph that is not improving, doing forty-five minutes of work on it because the card said so, and writing the next card, and repeating.

The paragraph eventually got better. It took about 11 months by the end. The chapter eventually became a chapter. Eighteen months after the worst stretch, the dissertation eventually became a dissertation. None of the becoming felt like becoming while it was happening.

That is the long middle. That is what nothing-visible looks like in practice.

The system held.

That is the chapter.

I want to give you a civilian version of this, because the eighteen months I described above are particular to me, and the structure is universal.

The composite I want to give you is built from a particular kind of reader I have heard from. The reader is six months into the framework. They have done the chapters. They have written the obligation list. They have started the verbs-not-titles practice. They have begun, in some form, the smallest thing worth building. They have picked a future-self practice. They have been running the Sunday audit for six months. They are, by every measure of *doing the system,* doing the system.

And nothing is happening.

The reader writes me, six months in, with a message that says, in some version: *I have been doing this for six months. The cards are being written. The audits are being filed. I am showing up. I am in motion. But I do not feel different. I do not see anything different. I keep waiting for the thing the book promised, and it does not seem to be arriving.*

I have, over the years, written some version of the same reply enough times that I want to give it to you here.

The reply has three pieces.

The first piece is: *what you are describing is the system working as designed.* The book did not promise that you would feel different at six months. The book promised that you would, by following the practices, *be* different at three years, at five years, at ten years. The feeling is not the metric. The feeling is downstream of the work, and downstream of the work, by years. At six months, the feeling will lag the work by some considerable distance.

The second piece is: *you have been undercounting your progress.* When I look back at my own eighteen-month stretch, I can see, in retrospect, that the period I called *nothing happening* was, in fact, full of small movements I had not been counting. The Boeing program survived a year of administrative paralysis with my hand on it. The league survived a difficult season with most of its families re-registering. The dissertation chapter, paragraph by paragraph, became a chapter. None of these, week to week, looked like anything. All of them, in retrospect, were the substance of the eighteen months. The reader who is six months in is, almost certainly, undercounting in the same way.

The third piece is: *keep going.* This is the least satisfying piece of the reply, and the one I most want you to hear. The framework does not have a shortcut for the long middle. The long middle is the long middle. The way through it is to keep doing the practices, keep writing the cards, keep running the audits, and keep showing up. The keep-going is the chapter.

Most readers, upon receiving the reply, are not satisfied with it. The reply does not promise them anything. The reply does not offer them a productivity hack that will shorten the long middle. The reply tells them what they already, on some level, know — that the work is the work, that the time is the time, and that the way out of the middle is through it.

Most of those readers, when I check on them a year later, have come out the other side of the middle into something they would not have predicted at six months.

That is what the long middle does when you stay in it.

I want to give you a different composite, because the *nothing-is-happening* reader is one kind of test of the framework, and the reader who *drops it entirely and comes back* is a different kind. The second test, in some ways, is the more important one.

Her name in this book is Diane. She is fifty-eight, two years past a quiet civil divorce. She started the framework in the spring after the divorce was final. She wrote the obligation list. She started the index card practice on a Sunday in March. She added the community channel in May (a literacy circle through her church) and the future-self channel in June (Italian, on her commute, forty-five minutes a day).

By October, the framework was the spine of her week. The card on the bedside table, the Sunday audit, the Tuesday hour at the church, the language practice on the commute. She would have told you, that fall, that the framework had given her her life back.

In November, she got a job offer she didn't expect — a senior operations role at a company that had been her best consulting client. The hours were going to be heavy in the first six months. She accepted on the assumption, with herself, that she could keep the framework running through the transition.

She could not.

The first two weeks consumed everything. The card slipped on a Tuesday and she did not write a new one Wednesday. The Sunday audit slipped the following weekend. The literacy circle slipped the second week of November. By December, the language app's notifications had become something she swiped away without opening. By January, she had not done any element of the framework in approximately ten weeks.

She did not, at the time, articulate what was happening. The framework was simply not in her life anymore. The job was. She was good at the job. The work was real and the people were good and the role mattered. But by mid-February she had begun to notice a particular quietness in her own head that she remembered from the season after the divorce. The system she had built to keep that quietness from becoming the dominant feature of her life had been disassembled by the job, and she had not noticed the disassembly until the consequences arrived.

She did the only thing she remembered the book saying to do.

She wrote a card.

It was a Tuesday night in February. The card on the bedside table was still the last card she had written in November — *call my sister.* She did not throw it out. She wrote a new card on top of it. *Call my sister again.*

She made the call the next morning. Her sister, who is patient, picked up on the second ring.

That was the return.

It was not a triumphant return. Diane did not, that night, pick up all three channels. She did not run a Sunday audit that week. She did not open the language app. She wrote one card, and the next night she wrote another card, and over the following six weeks the framework rebuilt itself, more slowly than the first time, in roughly the same shape.

The literacy circle came back in early April. The Italian came back in May, on a slower cadence. The Sunday audit came back when she found the November pages in her folder and added a March page next to them.

By summer, six months after the disassembly, the framework was running at roughly two-thirds of its previous intensity. Diane, with the benefit of having lost it once, had a different understanding of what she was running than she had the first time around. She understood, now, that the framework was not something you set up and ran forever. The framework was something you *returned to*, after seasons in which it disappeared, because the seasons were going to come whether you planned for them or not.

The return is what you actually do.

Most adults who run the framework for ten years run a version of Diane's arc — not perfect compliance, but durable return. The compliance is not the practice. The return is the practice. If you find yourself, six months from now or three years from now, in a season where the cards have stopped and the audits have lapsed, do not throw out the framework. Do not decide it was not for you. Do not write a long internal post-mortem about why you failed.

Write a card.

Let me say what is happening, mechanically, when *nothing-is-happening* is happening.

Most of the work of an adult life is invisible to the worker doing it.

This is not a poetic claim. It is a mechanical claim. The arc on which the work pays back is almost always longer than the arc on which the worker can perceive payback. A teacher in her fourth year cannot, while in her fourth year, see the effect she will have on the kid who will, in his fortieth year, write her a letter thanking her for the thing she said in February of his sixth-grade year that she does not, herself, remember saying. A founder in his second year cannot, while in his second year, see the effect his current product decisions will have on the customer who will, eight years from now, be using the company's tools to do work that neither of them can imagine. A coach in his third season cannot, while in his third season, see the effect he is having on the kid who is twelve and who will, at twenty-two, become a coach himself in part because of how the third-season coach showed him how a coach is supposed to be.

The arcs are real. The arcs are also structurally longer than the worker's perception window.

The worker, while inside the arc, has only one reliable way to assess whether they are still on the arc: whether they are *still doing the work*. The work is the only honest indicator. Results are a lagging indicator and almost always lag the work by a duration that the worker is not equipped to estimate from the inside.

Most adults, when assessing their own progress, rely on results. This is correct in environments where the feedback loop is short — assembly lines, sales calls, sports games. This is wrong in environments where the feedback loop is long — careers, communities, families, formation. In long-loop environments, using results as a progress metric will yield a chronically incorrect reading. The reading will tell the worker, week after week, that they are not making progress. The reading will be wrong. The work is making progress. The progress is not yet visible in the result-watching window.

It is worth saying, before we go further, that the long middle is not a *complete* absence of signal. The long middle is the absence of a *result-shaped* signal. There are other signals available, and the reader who looks for them in the right places will find them.

The signal that the work channel is on the arc, even when results are flat, is whether the *quality* of the work is improving. Not the visible output. The texture of the work itself. Are you making decisions you would not have made two years ago? Are you noticing things in the work that you did not notice before? Are you, in conversations with colleagues, saying things that, on examination, are sharper than what you would have said the year before? Those are the quiet signals from the work channel. They are not on a results dashboard. They are visible only if you know how to look for them.

The signal that the community channel is on the arc, even when nothing dramatic is happening, is whether the *relationships* are deepening. The parent at the field who, over three seasons, has gone from a stranger to a person you recognize to a person who texts you when their kid has a hard week. The neighbor at the library class who, by month four, knows your name and asks about your wife. The kid who waved his stick at you on the field. These are not productivity outputs. They are the quiet evidence that the channel is producing exactly what it produces.

The signal that the future-self channel is on the arc, even when the practice feels stalled, is whether you are *thinking differently.* Not whether you have produced something. Whether the way your mind moves has begun to incorporate the practice. The reader of philosophy who notices, in a Tuesday meeting, that the framing the team is using has a flaw, the philosophy training has equipped her to see. The pianist notices that her sense of time has begun to refine itself outside the practice room. These are downstream of the practice and are visible if you know what to look for.

Look for those signals. They are real. They are how you can tell, while inside the long middle, that the work is doing what the work does.

I want to give you the practical implications of this.

In the channels of work, community, and future self, you should not be using results to assess your own progress. You should be using *consistency.* The relevant question is not *what have I produced this week?* The relevant question is *did I show up this week.* The first question, asked weekly for years, will produce a reading of ongoing failure that is structurally inaccurate. The second question, asked weekly for years, will produce a reading of ongoing showing-up that is structurally accurate.

The Sunday audit is an instrument for asking the second question, not the first. The audit is not asking you what your results were this week. The audit is asking whether you met the practice in this channel. The audit is, in effect, the consistency tracker.

The reason readers undercount their progress in the middle is that the cultural air they breathe — productivity, optimization, content about ROI, LinkedIn updates, the bookstore's bias toward visible transformation — has trained them to use results as the primary metric. The training is wrong for the channels. The channels do not respond to a results metric. The channels respond to a consistency metric.

Use the consistency metric. The results will arrive. They will arrive on a schedule you do not control. You will be doing the work for years before they arrive. The work, carried out consistently over those years, is what produces them. There is no shortcut. There is also no need for a shortcut. Showing up is the entire engine.

That is what nothing-is-happening looks like, mechanically. The nothing is, in fact, nothing. Nothing is the work. The work is the only thing that has ever produced something that comes later.

You may have three objections forming. Let me answer them now.

The first objection is: *what if I really am just stuck? What if I am the rare person for whom the framework genuinely is not working?* I want to answer this carefully. The honest answer is that the chance you are the rare person is small, but not zero. Most readers who fear they are the rare person are not. Most readers who fear they are the rare person are six months in, which is exactly where everyone is at six months. The way to know whether you are a rare person is to keep going. At eighteen months, if the audits are clean, the practices are running, and nothing visible has appeared, we have a different conversation. At six months, the conversation we have is *keep going.*

The second objection is: *what if the framework isn't working?* The framework not working is, in almost all cases, a misreading of what working means. The framework works when you show up. Showing up is the framework. The framework is not, on its own, supposed to produce anything. The framework is the showing up. If you are doing the practices and they are running, the framework is doing what the framework does. The thing you are waiting for is downstream of that, and is on its own clock.

The third objection is: *how long do I keep going? When does this stop being the long middle?* I want to be honest about this. The long middle does not announce itself when it ends. The long middle ends in retrospect. You will, at some point in year three or year four or year five, look back and notice that the period that felt like the long middle is now visibly behind you, and that the channel has begun to produce visibly. That is when the long middle ended. You will not know, on the day it ended, that it ended. You will know, six months later, that it had ended. The honest answer to *how long* is *long enough that you should not be measuring.* The measuring is the problem. Stop measuring. Keep showing up. The middle ends when it ends.

The practice for this chapter is called the thirty-day showing-up audit.

It is a corrective practice. It is meant to be run when the Sunday audit produces low scores across all three channels, and the reader starts to suspect they are stuck. The thirty-day audit is the cure for the stuckness reading.

Take a piece of paper. Write at the top *the last thirty days.*

Now look back over the last thirty days and list, by date if you can remember, *every time you showed up consistently in any of the three channels.*

The list is, in most readers' cases, longer than they expect.

The work-channel showing up: the meetings you attended on time and prepared for. The calls you returned. The emails you cleared by the agreed deadline. The week you led the team meeting, even when you didn't feel like it. The quarter when you delivered the thing the role required.

The community channel showing up: the Saturday morning you went to the field, even when you didn't want to. The Sunday morning you taught the class because you said you would. The Tuesday you showed up at the literacy center. The friend you called when she was going through a hard time. The neighbor whose package you accepted.

The future-self-channel showing up: the practice sessions you did. The reading sessions you completed. The hour on the calendar you protected. The cadence you held even partially.

Make the list specific. Not *I worked.* The dates of the meetings, the names of the practices, and the specific Saturdays. The specific is more useful than the abstract.

When the list is finished, look at it. Most readers, when they do this, find that they have shown up — somewhere, in one of the channels, for some amount of time — almost every day of the past thirty. The narrative they had been telling themselves was *nothing is happening.* The narrative the list tells them is *I am showing up consistently in two of the three channels and intermittently in the third.* The two narratives are different. The second one is more accurate.

The thirty-day audit is the practice used to correct the misreading.

The misreading is the source of most of the despair that is generated by the long middle. The despair is downstream of the misreading. The misreading, on examination, is the result of using a results metric to assess work on a consistency arc. The thirty-day audit replaces the results metric with the consistency metric on a single page.

Save the page.

You will probably want it again.

——————————————

The reflection for this chapter is the thirty-day showing-up audit:

Look back at the last thirty days. List, by date or by week, every time you showed up consistently in any of the three channels — work, community, future-you. Be specific: the meetings, the Saturday mornings, the practice sessions, the calls. Read the list. Notice that you have been showing up. Save the page.

You may discover, when you do this, that the version of yourself you have been describing in your head — *nothing is happening, I am stuck, the framework is not working* — is not the version that the page describes. The page describes someone who has been showing up. The page describes someone in motion. The page describes a person who is doing the work even when the work is not being produced this week.

That person is you.

The framework is, by any reasonable measure, working.

You are in the middle. The middle is the chapter you are in.

Save the page.

——————————————

A note before we close.

You have just been given the most important orientation of this book.

The middle is the place where the system is supposed to feel like it is not working. The middle is most of the time. The work of the middle is to keep showing up, regardless of what the results metric is telling you, until the consistency metric eventually produces the results that the consistency metric has always produced.

The next chapter — the closing chapter — is about what the work has, in the end, been building.

That is Chapter 12.

Chapter 12 — What You're Building

I want to take you back to a kitchen.

The kitchen is the one we opened the book in. Renee. The mug. The robe. The microwave clock at 5:47. The Slack notifications that had stopped on day two. The way the body had still been trying to lead.

That was the opening of this book. I want to bring you back to that kitchen now, six months later, because the book is supposed to do something to a reader and I want you to see — by way of seeing what it has done to Renee — what it has done, in some structural way, to you.

It is a Wednesday in early autumn. Renee is in the kitchen. The robe is the same robe. The mug is the same mug. She still has the CHIEF MARKETING OFFICER mug, and she still uses it on most mornings, and she has, at some point in the last six months, decided that keeping the mug is not, as she once thought it might be, a sign that she has not let go. The mug is just a mug. She has let go. The mug stayed because it was hers.

The microwave clock reads 5:47.

The differences are hard to see at first. She is wearing the same robe. She is in the same kitchen. She is drinking from the same mug. The differences are small. The differences are also in the chapter you are reading.

The first difference is the phone.

The phone is not face down on the counter this morning. The phone is in her hand. There are three texts on the screen. Two are from a literacy program where she has been volunteering on Tuesdays for the last five months. One is from a younger woman she has begun to mentor through a women-in-marketing networking group she found on the third or fourth try after her old role ended. The texts are not work. The texts are not the kind of thing she would have used to fill the quiet six months ago. The texts are the small ordinary signals that, in some specific local way, she is being counted on.

The second difference is the calendar.

She has a Tuesday-afternoon block. She has a Sunday-morning audit ritual that takes about five minutes, and her husband has noticed it without commenting. She has a Wednesday-night practice — the cello she had played in middle school and had not touched in thirty-five years — that she does not, by her own choice, tell anyone about. She has, on the bedside table next to the lamp, an index card with tomorrow's next right step written on it in her own handwriting. The card was written last night before she went to sleep.

The third difference is the strangest one. She does not, on this Wednesday morning, have any specific idea of what the next ten years of her life are supposed to look like. She does not have a plan. She does not have a five-year strategy. She does not have a clearly named destination toward which she is, in some optimized way, moving.

What she has is a *direction*.

This morning, she is moving toward becoming a person in motion. She has not arrived. She is not finished. She is, however, no longer the woman she was on day nineteen, sitting in this same kitchen, in the same robe, holding the same mug, counting days.

That is the chapter you are reading.

Here is the chapter's claim, said plainly:

What you are building is not a destination. It is a direction.

The destination — the thing Renee was waiting for at the kitchen table on day nineteen, the thing the bookstore in the next aisle of the store has promised every reader for forty years — does not arrive. There is no day on which the work is finished. There is no ceremony at the end of an adult life that says: *here is the end of becoming. Here is the place where the long middle gives way to the long answer.*

The reason there is no such ceremony is that an adult life of any quality is not, structurally, organized around a destination. It is organized around a direction. The direction is composed of three channels that run in parallel: daily index cards, weekly Sunday audits, and the obligation engine underneath. The direction is not, on any given Tuesday, doing something dramatic. The direction is in motion every Tuesday.

The motion is the thing.

That is what the book has been about. That is what every chapter from the opening to this one has been pointing at. The reader who reaches Chapter 12 with the system in place is not a reader who has arrived. The reader who reaches Chapter 12 with the system in place is a reader who is *underway* — which is, as it turns out, the only durable thing an adult can be.

You do not get to feel done.

You get to be underway.

That is the chapter you are reading.

———————————————

Let me tell you what happened in Renee's six months, because the specifics are, again, more useful than the abstraction.

Month one was the hardest. She did the introduction. She read Chapter 1. She did the uniform inventory. She read Chapter 2. She did the honest accounting and noticed, in a way that made her sit with her coffee for longer than usual, how much harder the right column was than the left. She read Chapter 3 and put down the find-your-passion advice that had been killing her for nine months. She read Chapter 4 and made the list of obligations. She picked one obligation that morning and honored it before noon. The honoring did not change her life. The honoring did, however, change something in her head between 11:59 and 12:01, and the change was the first thing she had felt in three weeks that was not flat.

Month two was the practice month. She started the index card on March 4th. The first card said *call my sister.* She did. The second card said *send the email to Jennifer about the consulting project I have been avoiding.* She did. The cards have continued, every night, since.

In month three, she added the community channel. She walked into the literacy center on a Tuesday afternoon and asked if they needed a reader. They did. The first session was awkward. The second session was less awkward. In the fifth session, she had her first real conversation with the program coordinator, a woman about her age who, as it turned out, had been at the same college as Renee thirty years earlier and remembered her sorority's annual fundraiser. The coincidence was small. The conversation that followed it was not small. By the end of month three, Tuesday afternoon was a fixed point in her week.

In month four, she added the future-self channel. She picked the cello. She did not tell her husband for the first 30 days, as the chapter had told her to. By day thirty-one, she told him, and his only response was *I wondered what was going on.* He had noticed she had been disappearing into the spare room on Wednesday nights. He had not mentioned it. He had, in his own quiet way, been protecting the practice without being asked.

Month five was the long middle starting.

She noticed, in month five, that nothing in particular was happening. The literacy center was the same literacy center. The cello was producing exactly the kind of slow rusty progress that thirty-five-year layoffs from cello produce. The work channel was running but not, on any given week, producing anything she could put on a LinkedIn update. She had, on a Wednesday in month five, the first version of the *nothing is happening* feeling that the previous chapter had warned her she would have.

She wrote the thirty-day showing-up audit. She filled the page. She read the page. She noticed, on examination, that she had shown up — at the literacy center, in the cello practice, in the work channel, on the index cards — almost every day of the past thirty. The narrative she had been telling herself was wrong. The page told her so.

She kept going.

Month six is the month I am telling you about now.

On Wednesday morning, at the kitchen counter, with the mug and the phone and the calendar and the index card and the cello in the spare room. Nothing about that morning, by any external measure, is a triumph. There is no announcement. There is no celebration. There is no moment when her old colleagues call to tell her she has finally become someone they recognize again.

But she is, in that kitchen, on that Wednesday, *underway.*

The mug is still the mug. The robe is still the robe. The kitchen is the same kitchen. What has changed is the woman in it. She is not finished. She is in motion. She is a person who, on this Wednesday, has three specific channels of her life running, a daily practice that holds them together, a weekly practice that audits them, and a quiet, small, almost imperceptible sense that the cavity that woke her up on day nineteen has, somewhere in the last six months, become smaller.

It is not gone. It will probably not be entirely gone in this lifetime. The cavity is a consequence of the role ending, and that ending is not undone by the rebuild. The rebuild does not erase. The rebuild *refills* slowly over time with the substance of the new channels.

The substance is not visible from the outside. The substance is the kitchen at 5:47 a.m., the index card on the bedside table, the Tuesday afternoon block, the cello in the spare room, the literacy center on her calendar, and the obligation list in the drawer with the badge.

The substance is what you are building.

I want to give you my own current snapshot, since the book has been, for twelve chapters, at least partly about me, and the closing chapter is the place to be honest about where I am as the writer who has been writing it.

I am writing this chapter at home, at the same kind of kitchen table I have written most of this book on, on a Tuesday afternoon, in a stretch of my life that is not, by any external measure, a stretch of arrival.

The work channel is running. I have transitioned out of Boeing into a different role in an adjacent industry, doing work that, on most weeks, honors the duty I had been fulfilling. The work is not always satisfying. The work is real on most weeks.

The community channel is running. The lacrosse league is in its many-th season. I am no longer the head of it; that role has been handed to a younger man who is, by every measure, better suited to running it than I was at his age. I show up to the field on Saturday mornings as a kind of senior presence, the way the older men in the league I joined as a young father had once shown up on the fields where I was learning to coach. Some of the kids I coached at eight are now coaching the kids who are eight. The pass-forward is doing what the pass-forward does.

The future-self channel is running. I finished the doctoral program some time ago. The reading and writing have continued. The man I had imagined that night at the kitchen table is, in pieces, here. He is not finished. He continues to deepen in ways I did not anticipate when I started. The practice — reading, writing, sitting with hard texts, working slowly with ideas — is the practice. It will continue, on the same cadence, for as long as I am able.

I am not, at this stage of my life, *arrived.*

I am underway.

I want you to feel the difference, because that's what the whole book has been pointing to. *Arrived* is a destination. *Underway* is a direction. The men I know who used to be successful and are now, in their late sixties or early seventies, struggling with their own version of the cavity Renee was sitting with on day nineteen are men who organized their lives around arrival. They got to where they were going. They did not have, behind the destination, a *direction* that survived the arrival*.

The men I know who are seventy and are still in motion — still building, still practicing, still showing up at fields and libraries and community boards and synagogues and writing rooms — are men who, somewhere in their forties or fifties, made their lives about the underway rather than the arrived. They did not have a destination; they were chasing. They had three channels they were running, and they kept running them, and the running was, on examination, the entire architecture of who they had become.

I want to tell you what twenty years of running the three channels has actually changed about me, since the change is not, on most days, dramatic, and the closing chapter is the place to say it honestly.

The most important change is that I have stopped looking for a feeling I used to look for. The feeling I used to look for, in my thirties, was the feeling of *meaning.* I wanted, on most days, to feel that what I was doing meant something. The feeling came and went. The feeling was, on examination, an unreliable indicator of whether the work was meaningful. I have, over twenty years of running the three channels, stopped looking for the feeling.

What I have replaced it with is nothing. What I have replaced it with is *recognition.* On most days, in most channels, I can see that the work I am doing is recognizable as the work the version of me I am committed to becoming would be doing. The recognition is quiet. The recognition is not a feeling, exactly. The recognition is a small structural acknowledgment that I am, in this hour, in this conversation, in this email, doing the kind of thing the obituary I want would describe me doing.

That is the change. That is what twenty years of the system has done. The change does not announce itself. The change is not large on any given Tuesday. The change is, in aggregate, the difference between the man I was at forty-five and the man I am now.

If you keep running the system, you will eventually have your own version of this change. It will not look like mine. The shape of it will be yours. The mechanism by which it appears will be the same.

I am hoping to be one of those men. The hope is unfinished. The hope is what the work continues to be for. I will not, at this point, find out whether the hope is justified. I will keep working as though it is, until the work eventually stops, which it will, because everything eventually stops. The stopping is not the point. The work is the point.

The work is what you are building, too.

Let me say what the book has been arguing, in its most condensed form, so the closing chapter can leave you with it.

The book has been arguing that the cavity that woke you up at 5:47 a.m. on the morning the role ended is not a cavity that gets filled. It is a cavity that gets *replaced* — not by another role, but by a structure of running things that does not depend on any single role being in place.

The structure is the three channels. Work, community, future-self. Each one, alone, would not be enough. All three, together, form the spine of what an adult life with structural integrity looks like.

The engine is an obligation. Not motivation. Not inspiration. Not passion. *Obligation.* The specific, named, person-by-person, decided obligation of a person who has chosen to be useful to someone, and who shows up because they said they would.

The daily practice is the next right step. The card on the bedside table. The action before 10 a.m. The quiet keeping of small agreements with yourself.

The weekly practice is the Sunday audit. Five minutes. Three numbers. One decision about where the hour goes.

The corrective practice, when the long middle is producing despair, is the thirty-day showing-up audit. The list of every time you have shown up consistently in the last thirty days. The reading of the list. The recognition that you have been undercounting.

That is the system.

The system is not impressive. The system does not look like much on any given Tuesday. The system is what every meaningful adult life with any kind of resilience has been built on, whether or not the people inside those lives have ever named it that way. The system is the architecture of staying in motion when the wellness industry has stopped being able to help you, when the productivity hacks have run out, when the well-meaning friends have run out of advice, when the books in the next aisle of the store have stopped working, and when the only person left to keep you in motion is you.

You can keep yourself in motion. The system is how.

I want to say one more thing, before we close, because the chapter would not be honest without it.

You are going to lose at this. Periodically.

You are going to fail to write the index card on some night. You are going to skip the Sunday audit on some Sunday. You are going to let the literacy center slide for a few weeks. You are going to skip the cello for a month. You are going to come into a stretch of your life — illness, a parent's death, a difficult marriage, a hard year at work — that wipes out the cadence of the system you have built. The system will be in pieces. You will not know how to put it back together. You will, in some bad moment, wonder whether the framework was ever real.

It was real.

You will, in those moments, return to the practice. Not all at once. Not heroically. The way you return is the way you started: one card. One small action. One Sunday audit. One Tuesday afternoon at the literacy center. The return is the practice. The return is, more than anything else in the book, the thing the framework is engineered for.

The return is what makes the framework durable.

You will return many times in the rest of your life. The return is not a failure. The return is the system working as designed.

That is the architecture. That is what you are building.

You may have three objections forming. Let me answer them now.

The first objection is: *but I want a destination. I want to know where I am going.* I hear you. The desire for a destination is not silly. It is also, on examination, not what you actually want. What you actually want, if you sit with the desire long enough, is the *quality of being on the way to somewhere* — the sensation of forward motion, the sense that the days are accumulating into something, the feeling of being in a story whose chapters are still being written. That feeling does not require a known destination. That feeling requires a *direction.* The direction is what the system gives you. The destination is what the destination industry has been selling you, and the destination industry's product was not, on examination, the thing you actually wanted.

The second objection is: *this is just keep-going-forever. There is no end.* That is correct. There is no end. The good news, which the chapter has been hinting at since the opening, is that the no-end is not a threat. The no-end is what makes the arrangement durable. A life with an end state is a life with fragility built in. A life organized around being underway does not collapse when no end state arrives. The no-end is the strength of the system, not its limitation.

The third objection is: *when do I get to feel done?* You will not feel done. You will, however, feel underway. The feeling of being underway is not the same as the feeling of being done, but it is, in the lives of the men and women I have watched do this work, a more durable and more honest version of what most people thought *being done* would feel like. The wellness industry has trained you to look for *done.* The book is asking you to look for *underway.* The first is unavailable. The second is available to you on the morning you decide to take it, at this point in your life.

The practice for this chapter is called the obituary direction.

It is the only practice in this book that asks you to think on a longer arc than five years.

Take a piece of paper. (Last time. The same paper. The same pen.)

At the top of the page, write *the obituary I would be proud of.*

Now write the obituary. Not in the form of a CV. Not in the form of a list of achievements. In the form of a *portrait.* What is the duty you carried? Who were the people you served? What were the channels you ran for the last twenty years of your life? What version of you emerged from running them?

Be specific. Use names where you can. *He showed up for his sons. He stayed in his marriage when other men did not. He coached the U-12 team for eighteen seasons. He kept reading. He learned to speak the language he had wanted to speak since he was twenty. He died in motion.* Whatever your version is.

Write the version of yourself you would, in twenty or thirty years, be proud to leave behind.

When you are done, look at the page.

The page is your direction.

The page is not a plan. The page is not a destination. The page is, in compressed form, the version of you that the system you have built over the last twelve chapters points to. You will not, in the rest of your life, hit every detail of the obituary you have written. You will, however, be moving on most days in roughly that direction.

That is enough.

Now do one specific thing.

Look at the obituary. Pick one sentence on it that, on examination, is not yet true. *He stayed in his marriage when other men did not. He learned the language. He coached the team.* Whatever your version is.

Take one small action this week toward making that sentence true.

If the sentence is about marriage, take the action that is about the marriage. If the sentence is about the language, schedule the language session. If the sentence is about the coaching, send the email to the rec center.

Pick one. Take it.

That is the closing practice.

That is, in fact, the entire system, condensed into a single move the morning after you finish the book.

One more note about the obituary, before we leave the practice.

The obituary is not a one-time exercise. The obituary is something you will, if you let it, return to every two or three years for the rest of your life. The first version you write will probably be honest but partial — there are versions of yourself you have not yet imagined that the system, if you keep running it, will eventually let you imagine. The obituary you write at fifty will not be the obituary you write at sixty, and the obituary you write at sixty will not be the obituary you write at seventy. The shape will sharpen. The portrait will deepen. The you-on-the-page will be progressively more specific to who you have actually become.

That is what writing the obituary every few years is for. It is the long-arc check on whether the system is producing the person you set out to produce, and it is the one practice in this book that gets richer the longer you do it.

File the page. Find it again in three years. Read it. Notice what is and is not still true. Write the next version. Repeat for the rest of your life.

That is the practice that closes the book.

Save the page. We are done.

The reflection for this chapter is the obituary direction in its most condensed form:

Write the obituary you would be proud of in twenty or thirty years. Not a CV. A portrait. The duty you carried, the people you served, the version of you that emerged. Pick one sentence on it that is not yet true. Take one small action this week toward making it true. Save the page.

You may discover, when you do this, that the obituary you wrote describes someone who has been waiting for you to commit to becoming them. Most readers, when they let themselves write the obituary without filtering, find that the man or woman on the page is already legible — already named — and has been quietly waiting for you, for some considerable number of years, to take the work of becoming them seriously.

The work is the system. The system is what the rest of your life is for.

A note before the book ends.

You started this book in Renee's kitchen on day nineteen. You are finishing it in Renee's kitchen six months later, with the cello in the spare room, the literacy center on the calendar, and the index card on the bedside table.

You also started this book in your own kitchen.

I do not know your kitchen. I do not know the morning the role ended for you. I do not know the texture of your version of the cavity, or the specific people on your obligation list, or the verbs you performed in the title you wore, or the practice you have begun to choose. I know that you have, by reaching the back cover of this book, walked through twelve chapters of architecture for what comes after.

The architecture is now yours.

The system is now yours.

The morning after you put down this book, you will be in your own kitchen, with your own coffee, with your own version of an index card on the bedside table.

You do not have to feel ready.

You just have to take the next right step.

Tomorrow, take it again.

Conclusion — Tomorrow

The book is over.

The work is starting.

I want to give you, in the next fifteen hundred words, what you need to keep the system running for the rest of your life. Not a summary. You have read the chapters. You have the architecture. What you need now is a small portable version of the system that fits in a single coda, that you can reread on a Tuesday morning two years from now, when the cadence has slipped, and you cannot remember whether the framework is real, and that will return you to the practice in the time it takes to finish a cup of coffee.

That is what this is.

Three practical handoffs. One closing line. Then the book ends, and your version of the work continues.

Handoff 1: Keep an index card by the bed.

Every night before you sleep, write tomorrow's next right step on a card. One item. Small, specific, defensible, accountable to your future self. Put the card on top of your phone, on the bathroom mirror, or wherever you will see it before the day starts. In the morning, do the thing on the card.

That is the daily practice. It is, by itself, more than most adults are doing in any structured way for their own forward motion.

If you do nothing else from this book, do this. The card will, over a year, accumulate into a record of three hundred sixty-five small actions, almost all of which you will not remember writing, almost all of which produced a small movement, and the cumulative effect of which will be a life that has continued to move when most lives in your demographic have stalled. The card is the thing.

Some readers, after a few months, swap the index card for a sticky note or a small notebook. The form does not matter. The constraint matters. One thing. Small. Today.

If a card is missed, write the next one. The return is the practice.

Handoff 2: Audit the three channels every Sunday.

On Sunday morning, afternoon, or evening, your call — take a piece of paper. Write three column headings: *Work. Community. Future you.* Score yourself one to ten on each for the past week. Do not average. Look at the lowest score. Pick a thirty-minute action for the lowest channel. Take it before next Sunday. File the page.

Five minutes. Three numbers. One decision.

The audit is the structural piece that prevents the three channels from drifting unnoticed. Without it, one channel will, every six to nine months, quietly start to dominate the other two, and you will not notice until the imbalance has produced symptoms that look — to your eye, in the moment — like depression, burnout, or aimlessness, but are in fact only the predictable consequence of a starving channel.

The audit is the cheapest, most reliable diagnostic any self-managing adult has ever had access to.

Run it weekly. File the page. By the end of the year, you will have fifty-two pages and a clearer record of where your life has been than any productivity app has ever given you.

Handoff 3: Name one obligation each Monday morning.

Every Monday morning, before you check your email, name one obligation you plan to honor that week.

The obligation need not be on the formal list. The obligation need not be a big one. The obligation has to be a *specific, named, person-facing commitment* that you are choosing to honor this week, and that, if you do not name it now, will probably slide.

Call my brother on Wednesday night. Be on time for Daniel's Tuesday game. Send the thank-you note to my mother that I have been meaning to send for three weeks. Show up for the literacy hour on Tuesday with the kid I read with last week. Sit with my wife after dinner on Thursday without my phone.

One obligation. One week. Named on Monday morning. Honored by Sunday night.

This handoff is the lightest of the three, and the one most readers underestimate. The Monday-morning naming is the engine that prevents the obligation list from becoming theoretical. The list, sitting in a drawer with the badge, is information. The Monday-morning naming is what translates the information into next week's action.

That is the third practice.

Some readers, when they start the three handoffs together, want to know what to expect in the first thirty days. I will tell you.

In the first week, the cards will feel awkward. The Sunday audit will take longer than five minutes because you will be unfamiliar with the scoring. The Monday obligation will feel a little stiff on day one. By the end of the second week, the card will have become a habit, the audit will have become routine, and the Monday naming will have become the kind of small ceremony that lives at the top of your week.

By day thirty, you will not, on most evenings, remember a time when you did not write the card. The audit will be five minutes. The Monday obligation will be the first thing you do at your desk.

You will have begun to feel, in some specific local way, that you are *running* — that the days are accumulating into something, that the week has a structure your previous weeks did not have.

You will not, at thirty days, have arrived. You will be underway in thirty days.

That is what the first month produces. From day thirty onward, the system gets easier, more durable, and more useful. Run it.

You will not run this perfectly.

You will skip a card. You will miss a Sunday audit. You will, in some bad week, fail to honor the obligation you named on Monday morning. The system will be in pieces. You will think, in some private moment, that the framework was something you did for a few months and that it has now lapsed.

Two rules.

The first rule: do not throw out the previous cards, audits, and obligation pages. Do not pretend the framework was not real. Do not, in particular, decide that because you have lapsed, the framework "was not for you." The lapse is the test, not the verdict.

The second rule: write tonight's card. Run this Sunday's audit. Name this Monday's obligation.

The return is the practice. The return is, more than anything else in this book, what makes the system durable. The men and women I have watched do this work for years are not those who never lapse. They are men and women who *return* — without making a story about the lapse, without organizing the lapse into a verdict, without letting the lapse become the reason to stop.

The return is the system. Return.

Before we close, I want to give you a brief picture of what this looks like at the long end.

The men and women I know who have been running this system, in some form, for ten or fifteen years are people whose lives, on examination, do not look extraordinary from the outside. They have not, by their own account, become anyone they were not on the morning the role first ended. They are simply, on most days, still in motion. They are still showing up at the field. They are still keeping their language practices on Saturday mornings. They are still naming the obligation on Monday. They are, at sixty-eight or seventy or seventy-two, the people their grandchildren can count on. They are the people their younger colleagues call when something hard is going on. They are the people whose absence, when it eventually comes, will be felt — not because they made themselves into legends, but because they made themselves *useful*, across decades, in the small, specific local ways the system has been training you to be useful in.

That is what fifteen years of the system produces.

It is not glamorous. It is not viral. It is, however, the most honest version of a life well lived that I have ever been able to point at — and it is, structurally, available to you if you keep the cards going, run the audits, and name the obligations.

The book is your invitation.

That is the system in its portable form.

One card per night. One audit per Sunday. One named obligation per Monday morning. The three together produce a life in motion that, over the years, becomes the kind of life that the men and women you most respect have been quietly building, mostly without naming it.

You have everything you need.

You have the architecture from the twelve chapters. You have the three channels, the daily card, the weekly audit, the Monday naming, and the engine of obligation underneath. You have the practices this book has spent 50,000 words walking you through.

You also have a kitchen of your own, in which the morning the role ended is now some number of days behind you. The cavity is still there. It will probably never be entirely gone. The rebuild is your work. The work is what this book has been for.

Tomorrow morning, you will be in the kitchen.

The mug will be in your hand.

The card will be on the bedside table.

You do not have to feel ready.

You just have to take the next right step.

Tomorrow, take it again.

Acknowledgments

This book exists because of more people than I can adequately thank in a few paragraphs, but I want to name a few here.

To the coaches who showed up for me as a kid, and to the men who later showed up for the boys in our league: this book is, in some real sense, the long version of the thank-you I owe each of you.

To the squadron — to the wingmen, the maintainers, the crew chiefs, the operations staff who made every flight possible: I learned from you what I have spent the last twenty years trying to put on the page.

To the team at Boeing who took me in after the uniform came off and showed me how the work continued even when the cockpit was behind me: thank you for your patience and trust.

To my doctoral committee for your patience with a man who arrived at the program two decades older than he should have been, and for the work you put into the version of me that emerged.

To the beta readers who read drafts of this manuscript and pushed back on what was not yet honest, thank you for telling me the truth before the manuscript went to print.

To my wife, Claire, who has been at the center of every chapter of this book, even the ones that do not name her: every word here was made possible by you. Thank you for the kitchen, the patience, and the long view. I owe you most of what is good in my life.

To my children: I hope this book is, eventually, useful to you in some season I cannot yet predict. The duty I have tried to carry, in all its forms, has been carried for you.

And to the readers — the men and women I have not yet met who will hold this book on a Tuesday morning when their own role has just ended — thank you for picking it up. You are why it exists.

———————————————

About the author

Robby Allen is a former Marine Corps officer and F/A-18 pilot. After leaving active duty, he transitioned into the defense industry, where he spent several years working on systems that quietly affected the lives of pilots and operators he had once been one of. He founded a youth lacrosse league in his community and continues to show up at its games on Saturday mornings. He completed a doctoral program in his early fifties, not for the credential but for the version of himself he wanted to be at sixty-five.

He lives in Northeast Florida with his wife and three children. He writes a bi-weekly letter that goes deeper into the framework in this book — one essay every other Sunday morning — at **thenextrightstepbook.substack.com**.

He is still in motion.

A request

A small request before you go.

If this book mattered to you — if any chapter of it changed something in how you are running your week, or named something you had been carrying without language for it — I would be grateful if you would leave an honest review on Amazon. Not a long one. Two sentences are enough. Reviews are how a book like this finds the next reader who needs it, and the next reader is, on most days, the person this book was written for.

Thank you for reading. Take the next right step.

———————————————

Reading list — five books that shaped this one

These are five books that, in different ways, shaped the one you are holding. If any chapter of this book opened a door for you, the books below are where that door leads.

Man's Search for Meaning, by Viktor Frankl. The closest cousin to this book in spirit. Frankl's frame — that meaning is found in service to something larger than the self, even in the most reduced circumstances — is the philosophical bedrock of the framework you have just read.

So Good They Can't Ignore You, by Cal Newport. The clearest book ever written against the find-your-passion advice industry. If Chapter 3 of this book worked for you, you owe Newport a careful reading.

Grit, by Angela Duckworth. The empirical case is that passion is developed, not discovered, and sustained over the years through practice. A useful companion to Newport and to the build-model from Chapter 3.

The Second Mountain, by David Brooks. The book this book is, in one sense, in conversation with — Brooks's framing of the second-half-of-life pivot toward commitment is well-aligned with what Part III is asking you to do.

What Are People For?, by Wendell Berry. Essays on useful work, place, and community, written in the slowest and most patient prose

I know. Read one essay a week. The book will deposit something on you that no productivity manual ever will.

That is enough.
Begin tomorrow.